THE TIBETAN YOGAS OF DREAM AND SLEEP : THE TIBETAN PATH OF SPIRITUAL AWAKENING

Guide to Mastering Your Dream Life Through Lucid Dreaming With Step-By-Step Instructions

Tibetan Yoga Academy

Disclaimer

All erudition contained in this book is given for informational and educational purposes only. The author is not accountable for any results or outcomes that emanate from using this material. Constructive attempts have been made to provide accurate and effective information, but the author is not bound for the accuracy or use/misuse of this information.

Table of Contents

IDIOTICON...1

INTRODUCTION 2

Receiving, Understanding, and Applying the Teachings 5

PART ONE...7

THE ESSENCE OF DREAM 7

Relationship between Dreams and Actual World 7

How Actions Affect Dreams 8

Ignorance and Duality 10

Deeds and Effects: Wyrd And Karmic Traces 12

Positive and Negative Karmic Forces 14

Liberating Emotions 16

Dream and Karma..18

The Six Dimensions of Possible Existence..21

Why Not Positive Emotions? 33

Cultivation, Dissipation, and Interaction with Energy Flow 35

Karma and Prana 40

PART TWO 46

TYPES AND APPLICATIONS OF DREAMS. 46

Types of Dreams 46

Application of Dreams...........................51

Dreams, Directions, And Divination..........52

Uncovering the Bon Practice of Chod.........56

PART THREE....................................64

THE YOGA OF DREAMS IN PRACTICAL
SENSE...64

Perception, Behavior, Dream, And Death ..64

The Art of Calm Abiding (Zhine)..............68

The Four Basic Yogic Practices..................78

How to Prepare For The Night..................90

The Ultimate Practice Of 'Guru Yoga' 96

The Principal Practices in Dream Yoga.....100

Order of Practice...............................116

Developing Your Capability of Lucid
Dreaming.......................................122

Attaining Suppleness 129

Hindrances Associated With Dream Practice
....142

Recognizing, Managing, And Utilizing
Dreams 147

Simplification Of Sleep And Dream Yoga.153

Unification of All Practices 159

PART FOUR 167

THE CONCEPT OF SLEEP 167

    Losing Oneself To Sleep............................167

    Practical Teachings Of Sleep And Dream .175

PART FIVE 183

PRACTICING SLEEP YOGA 183

    The Guardian of Sleep 183

    The Preparatory Practice............................189

    Main Practices During Sleep.......................192

    Stages of Sensory Withdrawal 196

    The Glowing Ball..201

    Development In Practice 204

    Associated Hindrances...............................207

    Practical Recommendations........................213

    Unification Of Rigpa..................................221

CONCLUSION 235

IDIOTICON

Dakini: A female spiritual being that appears to yogis in dreams for several purposes.

Prana: The energetic component of the body.

Chakra: An energy point located in a specific part of the body.

Bardo: The intermediate state after death.

Zhiné: The state of absolute calmness.

Tiglé: An energetic sphere of light.

Guru yoga: The practice of merging the mind with The Master's.

INTRODUCTION

Sleep is like a snare that captures everyone in the end, no matter who we are or what we do. We all go about our activities daily, some of us making things happen while others are at the receiving end. However, when the day ends and night falls, we all shut our eyes and go to sleep. A series of events then start to occur after that moment which the conscious mind is no longer in control of. As we then progress deeper into sleep, we travel through several dimensions in the entirety of the vast dream world. We undergo each of these discretely mysterious processes every night. Yet, we make no meaning whatsoever of these occurrences. Sleep, as most people would presume, is not precisely a one-sided experience. What if our supposedly real life is actually another form of sleep and dream? The essence of dream yogas is to enlighten us to the truth as we begin to appreciate and tread the path to profound meditation.

To realize one's true state of mind has been the primary fulfillment of different great Lamas and Yogis for many centuries. They have been faced with obstacles; they have conquered and acquired the same spiritual state accessible to any determined yogi. The appreciation of the teachings of the people from whom the knowledge was passed will further intensify our belief in the overall spiritual doctrine.

Before recent times, the teachings have been considered a sacred practice and were just not available at the disposal of ordinary people who have no basic understanding of what the teachings entail. This is to keep the respect and virtue of the teachings in place and away from the irrelevant changes that inexperienced learners might have made. We live in an ever-changing world and although, it is important to take serious note of the overall importance of the teachings, keeping the information from being generalized will not, in any way, intensify its value. Hence, I am making it available with the hope that prepared practitioners assimilate its worth and value. When furthering the practices on a personal note, it is advisable to use an experienced oral instructor who can help identify and overcome obstacles that would have proved challenging to overcome when practicing alone.

The human mind is a mighty one. The power to go on with life, to face the uncertainty of what is to come, the ability to analyze things to the most subtle detail are all the qualities of our human mind that cannot be found anywhere else in the universe. At every living moment, the inevitability of death gnaws at us. We are also aware that to prepare for the state after death (bardo) efficiently, one has to be a fully accomplished dream yogi. But we find it difficult to dedicate a reasonable amount of time to meditation. That brings us to the concept of Sleep and Dream Yoga, where we can learn how to use the time we spend sleeping for practice. Here, we will be learning how we can enhance our state of mind and create greater awareness to guide us throughout every moment of our lives by literally practicing and sleeping simultaneously. This book is mainly for helping us attain complete freedom and accomplishing a more genuine state of our minds, thereby unleashing full awareness both in dreams and in waking state. When fully enlightened, our mind will experience and appreciate its maximum ability in attaining regular, constructive, and spiritual freedom.

Using the teachings, we have discovered several ways to develop our lives' quality above the ordinary sense. We undergo the developmental processes with the help of these yogas. To achieve those ends, this book, if used as a practical guide, coupled with the crude knowledge from a qualified teacher, would be the best option.

The entirety of the human race has erred in delusions since time began. The vanity of samsara and habitual sufferings have lured man away from attaining notable forms of spiritual enlightenment. The teachings in this book are such that, if followed, they could lead and guide you to spiritual enlightenment. Such enlightenment will improve your ability to stay present when sleeping, increase your chance of attaining freedom and guide you to achieve higher spiritual achievements. You will, after that, find yourself relating with your experiences while sleeping and ultimately preparing for what is to come after death (bardo).

Receiving, Understanding, and Applying the Teachings

The process of learning about teachings like this one can either be in oral or written form. But the actual learning should not stop only when the concept is fully understood. Instead, we should apply the knowledge in physical practice. Only then is learning incessant and considered valuable.

When receiving the teachings, there is no good or bad student. There is only the strength and power of the mind and will. The strong-willed student is like a bucket. Whatever you put inside will stay there, no matter the circumstance. The weak-minded student is like a sieve. Everything you pour into it will come out the other way no matter what you do. The student should hold on firmly to the teachings, reflect on them and absorb them to full understanding.

When it comes to applying the teachings, we find that only what has been fully understood at the initial stages can be used in actual practice. It is like converting real-time knowledge into patent experience. It is practically unfeasible to completely grasp the message of the teaching unless you get to experience it first-hand. However, as trivial as that may seem, one should not just store up teachings as residual knowledge without intellectual understanding and complete assimilation. The teachings are not only meant to be stored but to be put into practice.

PART ONE

THE ESSENCE OF DREAM

Relationship between Dreams and

Actual World

A dream is a natural projection of the human brain's fantasies that takes place only when we are asleep. Everyone dreams, even though we might not remember the dream, and we will continue to dream till we die. During dreams, we may find ourselves to be somewhere familiar or in a strange place instead. We may see people we know or the ones we don't, we may do ordinary or extraordinary things, or we may even dream just to watch other people. For the ordinary mind, these are things that we exhibit no control over. But for a mind that has been polished with meditation and sharpened by the practice of spiritual teachings, dreams are just as good as any waking hour. Although dreams have raised the attention of curious minds worldwide, many only pay attention to the happenings in a dream and the meaning of such a dream. Very few people wonder about the essence of the dream itself. We get carried away by the contents of a dream instead of trying to delve into the subtlest nature of the dream.

To become a successful dream practitioner, it is essential to understand that dreams represent great value in learning the fundamental teachings. It is also crucial to realize that the concept of tagging a dream as unreal is very wrong indeed. The truth is that dreams are as real and vital as the regular waking hour, and it is not until you fully understand this that you can become a prepared dream yogi.

How Actions Affect Dreams

To be fair, our feelings and actions affect how we reason and, subsequently, what we say and do. For an ordinary mind, feelings play a large part in deciding what one's dreams will be all about. When you go to sleep with an emotion-laden head, you are likely to encounter things in your sleep that are similar to your experiences concerning the particular emotions with which you slept.

We are governed by the environment in which we find ourselves. Our mentalities are trapped and confined in the limits of our civilization. We are at war with our inner selves and place the blame on the environment. The sole cause of our suffering is not from the environment we live in; it is instead from the greed and discontent that we house in our minds, wishing that things were different with us. Unless we get rid of the innate desire, it will forever follow us wherever we go. If we don't understand this, we would be tossed back and forth without having a single means of escaping the fear and turmoil that lingers in our unenlightened minds. Our several forms of delights are the causer of the strife in which we have found ourselves. We develop an interest in things based on preferential values; we act only because of ourselves and not because of others; we hold several beliefs contrary to that of others and make the world and hold contrasting feelings for one another.

There is, however, another form of belief that arises from the imperfection of different cultures. In this case, indifference has been systematized and developed into our ways of life over a period of time. These particular beliefs are not basic; they are the rather dubious parts of culture.

Ignorance and Duality

If we consider all apparent factors, it would be right to say confidently that our affinity with all the vastness and vanity of the samsara (world) actually evolved from the biformity of our minds. We tend to believe in the doubleness of the forces that rule the universe. We base all our cultures on the fundamental beliefs that denote the existence of two opposing forces of good and evil, right and wrong, the universe and nothingness. These fragments of beliefs toggle our senses to create diversions towards the enticing affection of Samara (the world). Our inability to process and digest the true nature of the world is not entirely our fault. It is just the way we are. Over the years, we have been inclining further away from intense spiritualism. The results are everywhere, even in the ways we are taught. All our lives, we have been taught to look in the mirror, to live in ignorance. Instead of relating to life as it really is, we take the wrong side for the right one, thus attaining a high sense of precision and near perfection in the fallacious field. None of these is terrible, however. We are just who we are, regardless of what sorts of teachings we receive. It is not our fault that we were born into a particular culture or made to embrace certain beliefs; it is just that the more ignorant we are, the further away from attaining enlightenment we become. There is a particular saying in Tibet that goes thus, "When in the body of a donkey, enjoy the taste of grass." That implies that this life is conceptually significant, no matter what sort of cosmic attainment we get the chance to possess. Not appreciating it is just another means of escalating our ignorance.

When observed from a subtler form of view, dualism must be used as a supportive attachment with the teachings in the process of embracing spiritual strength and warding off vulnerability. This is a very vital objective when treading the path to enlightenment. Hence, there is a very high possibility of making mistakes. That is why it is so important to practice.

Deeds and Effects: Wyrd And Karmic Traces

As humans, we exhibit a tendency for desiring both essential and non-essential desires. We do things as we see fit and get fed up with things easily. It is all in our nature of being human. We may develop the need to possess some material objects and, after getting them, cultivate a pristine desire for new and better ones. The discontent and greed are just some of the hassles we encounter in the form of feelings and temptation, no matter how hard we try to escape from it. We feel the need for change, the need to possess, to adore the wide varieties of things offered by the samsaric (worldly) realm. From these kinds of feelings arise actions. We take actions as a result of what we feel. These actions, however, affect our lives and the way we live them in certain ways. This is the starting concept of wyrd.

We do things, and we take actions based on what we feel. These actions pave the path for our karmic results. Therefore, it is believed that karma is a factor that influences our future, including the way we react to conditional outcomes.

In a literal sense, Karmic traces are how our actions haunt us to produce the natural outcome based on previous occurrences. Our deeds never go unnoticed by karma, the supposed guardian of the cosmic world. This goes by the saying, "No matter how fast a man runs, he can never run past his karma." This is a considerable guide to understanding the somewhat cumbersome way of the universe. Regardless of its nature, as long as it leads to acknowledgment or repulsion, our reaction to different occurrences determines the karmic state of our minds. Karmic traces of our past actions cause every reaction we make, these reactions further initiate more karmic results, and these results are reacted to, once more, courtesy of karma. This is how we repeat karma all over again without even meaning to. When things continue this way, there is no cessation of deeds and effects. It is the wheel of samsara.

Although we may perceive the world's dynamism in different ways, every pizzazz and dimension in the world are governed by this same idea of karma. From the seemingly vaguest form of reality to the vast fragments of experience in the universe, all are conditioned and manifested by karmic forces.

There are conditions and specific periods to be met for every single trace of karma left in the mind before they can manifest. Karmic imprints are, in some ways, similar to the nature of human behavior. Just as some particular conditions and situations are required to uncover a person's true nature, karmic traces deposited in the mind also require the perfect situation to manifest. In other words, for Karmic traces to be released in the form of a result, there are certain conditions (secondary conditions) to be met. However, it is feasible to annul new karma from forming from our emotions by allowing it to self-liberate. Once we really understand this principle of deed and effect, instead of creating experiences that will negatively affect us, we can let ourselves be overwhelmed by positive experiences.

Positive and Negative Karmic Forces

The kind of reaction you put into the world goes a long way in determining the type of karmic trace that will be left behind in your mind. If you react to any experience in a negative way, the negative karmic trace is left in your mind. When the conditions for payback are perfect, you will encounter experiences that once more require adverse reactions, making it more likely for the negative emotions to rise within you with each experience karma brings forth. For example, if someone hates you and you respond by developing a similar hatred for the person, the karmic trace that is left within your heart will make you liable to develop fresh hatred for someone else that you think deserves it. Again, we become more susceptible to encountering such secondary conditions that make the hatred rise again. This becomes a habitual emotion. People with negative feelings and emotions like anger and hatred will always encounter situations that justify their negative feelings and emotions.

There are ways to use positive karmic forces to counteract the negative karmic forces' effect. For example, instead of responding to negative forces with the same kind of karmic energy, we can actually try to initiate a positive remedy to annul the negativity. For example, if we know someone that hates us and if we feel the need to respond with hatred, we should, in any case, remember that the remedy is love. Self-stimulating may feel ingenuine or false, but if we try to perceive that person's perspective, we would understand that they are overwhelmed by their own negativity. By so doing, we start to build positivity inside of ourselves.

Understanding this procedure in its entirety will make it much easier to embrace positive karmic traces. So, the next time we come across people with negative emotions, we are more likely to respond positively. By continuing in this way, it becomes a practice, and positive emotions will autonomously be spawned without considerable effort. This makes us more likely to make positive decisions and encounter positive experiences in the samsara (world). Eventually, the positive emotion becomes a part of us, making us less and less likely to respond to the contrasting situation with negativity.

Liberating Emotions

Whenever we are faced with the difficulty of determining the best way to respond to negative feelings, that is to say, a better way than generating positivity in our mind, self-liberation becomes a matter of utmost importance. We allow emotions to self-liberate by embracing and holding on to a state of non-dual awareness, without the feeling of acknowledgment or repulsion. However difficult this might prove, being able to pull it off over and over again makes us immune to the impact of emotions. It goes straight through us without leaving any new traces, just like a bird gliding through the air. We feel the emotion steadily rise within us, but then it autonomously vanishes without a trace.

Although we let out the liberating feeling as a thought or in the form of physical actions, we should not attach any response of acknowledgment or repulsion; we avoid the creation of future karmic traces. In your mind, when you self-liberate negative emotions like envy or anger, the strength of the karmic force associated with that particular feeling becomes jeopardized. So, as we self-liberate negative emotions into nothingness, we weaken karmic forces without us feeling any acknowledgment or repulsion. Finally, the mind breaks free from karma to its near entirety. It will be as though we destroyed the seed of karmic seeds before they have any chance to germinate into results.

The nature of all karmic traces is to try and restrain us from attaining emotional freedom. Hence, letting emotions self-liberate is a better option than creating positive karma, which still leaves behind a karmic trace, even though it is a positive one. Here, we work towards general self-liberation; positive emotions like love are not affected, however. They are still very much present in our minds, but with self-liberation, we try to erase all karmic traces, and this enables us to react to situations in the best manner, therefore helping us make the right choices.

This process of allowing emotions to self-liberate is the best way to respond to any form of negative karmic traces, but it requires high-level practice. Although you must have developed your practice level to get it right, you can still set determination. When emotions arise, you should relax as much as you can, check your internal balance, and then act as calmly as possible, without actually forcing it. Everyone can understand to control their outburst of emotions and thereby lessen the effect of habitual karmic forces.

Even as you start to adopt the process of emotional self-liberation, there will still be some leftover karmic traces in your mind. These are known as residual karmic traces. It is then up to you to remind yourself that those emotions result from the karma left in your mind. Afterward, when you deal with karmic traces, you do so neither by acknowledging nor repulsing the emotion. On a final note, the idea that every reaction to experiences (whatever its nature is) has its own result is a straightforward yet cumbersome one and, when fully understood, can help in the process of living a better life.

Dream and Karma

The way we feel about things and the way we react to them are controlled by karma. It shapes all our samsaric (worldly) experiences; the unity of karmic traces governs the sadness, the trust and love you feel for people, and envy. For example, you may sleep the previous night feeling okay, then you wake in the morning, feeling disgusted by something you cannot quite identify. The feeling further irritates you as it prolongs into the depths of your new samsaric (worldly) experiences. In this case, it is said that it is some mature karmic trace ready to manifest. It means that the conditions have become perfect for it to manifest into its own form of results. This may be happening for several reasons. There are also some ways karma may manifest, including during the night, in our dreams.

When an ordinary mind is asleep, our conscious mind, which creates short-lived feelings and ephemeral images, is absent, unable to restrain or annul the karmic traces. To effectively understand this, we need to realize that our consciousness lightens up our perceptive senses during the waking period of the day. We experience all the physical and psychical wholeness as a single string that makes up our life. At night, however, we lose consciousness, and the karmic traces manifest as a dream. If we have developed an excellent lucid practice, with much experience in this incredibly pure state of mind, our awareness will not be hindered in this state of lucidity. For the ordinary and weakly trained mind, the consciousness is left in a Cimmerian state while we experience dreams in the form of karmic trace manifestation.

The fragments of events that occur during dreams and sleep are like a photographic film that gets developed during the unawareness and darkness of our sleep. The most recently met perfect conditions determine the particular fragment of karmic traces previously deposited in our experiences that will be developed each night. Furthermore, in the same way, that we react to situations with variable intensities and in different manners, some karmic films are imprinted deeper into our minds than others, depending on how intense or powerful the action resulted in them. So, when the perfect conditions are met for a particular string of developed films of experiences to be manifested, it occurs as a dream that supports our humane definition of meaning.

When we encounter karmic experiences during dreams, we understand the basis in a more subjective way than observing physical life experiences. This is because we have an increased chance of expanding our restrained identities in the dream world. There is an absence of samsaric (worldly) factors and limitations that influence our physical world practice. Therefore, dream yoga's essence is to utilize dreams to cultivate a broader range of awareness and develop our minds' ability to make the right and positive choices. We train and alter our minds to respond with reactions different from the natural ones when faced with a negative experience. This creates new conductive karmic traces that, when mature, can be used for future dream practices. When the mind is trained to some certain extent, every experience you encounter will be seen as a chance for you to initiate the practice of feeling and reaction outburst. From there, you sharpen your mind and begin to exhibit enhanced awareness, thereby improving your ability to abide in awareness when dreaming and while performing other practices related to spiritualism.

When we practice during dreams, we get exposed to other ways of destroying the seeds that may give rise to future karma while still in the dreaming state. Self-liberation of emotions is also possible in dreams, but one must have a very high sense of insights and awareness to attain that.

The Six Dimensions of Possible Existence

There exist six different forms of existence in periodic dimensions. According to the teaching, each dimension has its own kind of cynical beings and its own articulation of negative emotion. These emotions manifest as Anger, Fear, Ignorance, Envy, Pride, and Distractive Pleasures. We sometimes possess each of these emotions singly or in a combined form. Distractive Pleasures is the combination of all other five, in absolute moderation. However, these dimensions are not just subjective to emotional feelings. They contain beings— different kinds of beings, ranging from humans' finest to the deadliest of hellish creatures.

We experience all sorts of emotions and samsaric trials here, in the human realm. Therefore, it is not challenging to understand that it will be so for all other realms, depending on their individual fundamental basic emotion. For example, the realm whose basic negative emotion manifests in us as anger, the hell, will contain many experiences that all segregate from anger and hatred. So, it should not be surprising to realize that the beings that reside in hell will be violent ones, exhibiting behaviors that support all the negativities related to anger. That is how it is for all other dimensions.

The realms are made of manifestations of karmic traces; just like it is in dreams, only that, in this case, the karmic traces are not experienced in the form of individuality but rather in an aggregate form. Thus, the beings in every realm share similar experiences, just in the same way we share experiences with other humans. Aggregated forms of karmic experiences create a gateway that forces all beings to share certain emotions and other categories of potentials in a particular realm. At the same time, it is practically impossible to participate in other kinds of experiences. For instance, animals can collectively see and hear things that humans cannot, and humans have the ability to understand a wide variety of things in a way animals cannot.

Our perception of the world, our world as real and corporeal, is a false one. In actuality, all the realms, including the human realm, are as insubstantial as the train of our thoughts and emotions—all the dimensions interconnected with one another and the beings who reside within. When our time runs out and the inevitability of nature finally unfolds (and we die), there is an equal possibility of our rebirth into each of the other realms. We carry a part of each realm with us. Whenever we get caught in a bout of negative emotional experience, we are being affected by the qualities of the fundamental elements of the other realms. When negativities like egoism or furious jealousy consume us, for instance, we are being affected by the karmic experiences from the demi-god dimension.

It is possible for a person to possess a predominance of one realm in their core. One can be more of a demi-god, more god nature, more animalistic in nature, or more of a hungry ghost. It occurs as a prevailing characteristic, and it can be acknowledged from the person's outward behaviors, like how they react to various forms of experience. When a person possesses more of the dominant trait of the hungry ghost realm, they never seem to have enough of anything. They are always overridden by the desire to get more. More of riches, more from the people around them; in other words, they can never be satisfied by anything. This possession of the predominant trait is, however, not very common. For most people, the traits from all the realms are blended in their nature. This proves how truly vast these realms are in the sense of their individual karmic experience.

These negative emotions are not necessarily meant to be confined to the separate realm from which it segregates; they can be experienced in every realm as karmic results, thereby making them universality apparent. The dimensions are also made up of a wide variety of karmic experiences, so it is pointless to determine which realm a particular feeling or emotion belongs. It would help us think of these conscious experiences as the trails that will guide us to our next life or reincarnation. For us to be born in a particular realm, our previous life must have been based on that realm's fundamental qualities of consciousness. That is considered the overall karmic results of our actions. For instance, to be born as a demi-god, one's previous life must have been lived based on the fundamental negative emotion of the demi-god realm (envy). As a natural alternative, the rebirth may be physical or staged in one's consciousness, in which case it is psychological. In psychological rebirth, we experience karmic traces that categorize us as beings from a different dimension, based on the particular negative emotion.

For most people, however, these negative emotions appear enticing. A person can be led into the extremities of negativities that they tend to get attracted to it. It is all the workings of karma. Our senses can become adapted and drawn to the negative emotions when we make ourselves vulnerable. Besides karma, other factors like culture and ignorance can also make a person feel inclined towards negative emotions. We say "stupidity is a virtue of animals," yet most of us are far from attaining true wisdom.

Some people may think of the existence of the six realms as some figments of our imagination. Still, if we pay attention closely enough, we would be able to identify the signs of karmic experience manifesting in our reactions to karmic situations. Sometimes, we just feel pure, unprecedented anger; we respond violently to everything around us, and the manifestation of karma in the behavior of the people around irritates us. At that very moment, we may be going through phases of karmic experiences from the hell realm. When we experience the emotions from these dimensions, our self-awareness must be withdrawn to avoid living too deeply in these moments of temporary douceur so that, when it eventually ends, we would not be adversely affected. For example, when you have a lovely weekend with your friends and family, upon getting back home, you feel somewhat depressed.

There are also times when you feel the different experiences of the realms. You can experience the emotions of the god realm (happiness) when you are with loved ones, while at other times, the experience of dullish ignorance overpowers your mind.

The negativities of all these realms also affect us while dreaming. In fact, the composition of a dream is connected to the reality of at least one of the six dimensions.

Hell

The fundamental emotion of the hell dimension is anger. The maturation of karmic wrath can manifest in various occurrences like hatred, violence, mercilessness, and cruel indifference. In our world, most wars' sole cause is anger, which only results in massive destruction and many deaths. But anger only brings torment and sufferings, never a peaceful settlement. When we get consumed by anger, we lose our self-consciousness and become overcome by the offspring of rage, thus taking part in the hell realm experience.

According to tradition, the hell realm is said to be made up of nine divisions of vast coldness and another nine divisions of extreme hotness in a single dimension. This means great punishment to the beings who reside therein. They are said to experience significant pain and distress, dying of immense measures of tortures and immediately coming back to life, back to eternal sufferings.

The center of energy for anger is the soles of the feet, and its remedy is absolute and unfettered love, which can only be attained with the body of pure awareness.

The Hungry Ghost (Preta) Realm

The fundamental emotion of this dimension is greed. Greed is basically a feeling of wanting and needing to fill the void we have created. For an ambitious mind, when we have all the wealth in the world, and we still wish for more, that is greed at work. Yet, we really desire to discover the secrets of our true nature, but we do not realize that fact.

The center of energy for greed is the chakra at the back of the genitals; hence greed is related to sexual desire. The remedy for greed is the state of candor and liberality. Honestly, giving out to the needy opposes the emotion of greed. Historically, the pretas (hungry ghosts) are described as beings with large bellies filled with painful emptiness, making them feel hungry all the time. They are also said to possess tiny mouths and throats. Some of them live in drylands that, according to the teachings, have not contained water for centuries. The others may settle in a place with some food and drink, but even if they manage to take in a tiny amount of food with their minute mouth and throat, upon entering their stomachs, the food bursts into flame, causing great suffering and torment for them. The pretas (hungry ghosts) encounter countless pains and distress, but every single pain results from their withholding of things that would have been beneficial to others. They suffer endlessly because of their avarice and niggardliness.

Animal realm

The fundamental negative emotion of this realm is ignorance. Ignorant beings experience this as a feeling of dullness, confusion, or foolish uncertainty. Associated with the darkness of ignorance are sadness, unawareness, stupidity, and lack of visual and psychological brilliance. Like all humans, humans who are entrapped by this emotion feel the need for samsaric excellence, yet they cannot find what to do to achieve it. Some people believe that busyness is equivalent to happiness, but we can still be consumed by our own ignorance while being busy. This feeling arises from our inability to discover our true nature.

The center of energy for greed is the chakra (energy point) at the center of the body, just at the navel level. The remedy for this emotion is reflecting inwards and finding truth and wisdom within oneself.

The realm of animals is ruled by the karmic feelings of ignorance and stupidity, and so are the beings that reside in it. Animals live in constant fear of being harmed or killed by humans and/or other animals. Animals suffer in several ways, from being hunted down and killed by the fiercest of humans to being perturbed by the gentlest of flies. Yet, most animals have become domesticated, beaten, milked, ridden, and made to work rigorously, all against their will, courtesy of human beings. Ignorance imprisons animals' minds and restricts them from searching beyond the mind's surface towards recognizing their true self.

Human realm

The fundamental negative emotion of the human realm is envy and jealousy. This emotion pushes us to feel bad whenever we think the people around us are getting successful. Instead of being content, we fill ourselves with jealousy and wish for things based on what we feel we need at the moment. We prioritize the objects, the affections we receive, the samsaric experience's ideas, and think of them as our path to happiness. In contrast, we are just forcing our minds further away from the truth.

Being our own very realm, it is not difficult to recognize our own sufferings and pains in the human realm. We age continuously till our time finally runs out. During the period in-between life and death, we attempt to acquire possessions like wealth and riches, and when we do, we dread its inevitable loss. Instead of appreciating and admiring the goodness that has happened to others, we entertain the presence of envy and jealousy within our minds.

The center of energy (chakra) for jealousy is the heart region. And to annul it, our minds have to be pure, open, and absolute in its entirety, the kind of attainment that we achieve when we find our true selves.

The Realm of Demi-Gods (asuras)

In this realm, the seed emotion is pride. The demi-gods see themselves as the solution to the problems of others. Thus, lost in their own selfish dignity, they often tend to go to war with one another, claiming to be just as good as the other.

The energy region for pride is the chakra in the throat. More often than not, experiences based on the stakes of pride lead to war; thus, the remedy for pride is faith and our ability to embrace humility. Only when we have discovered our true nature can we attain calmness even in the face of the pride and wrath of others.

The asuras can feel enjoyment and ample sufficiency, but as their nature supposes, they often declare war on one another to protect their pride and prove their superiority. That is just a piece of their sufferings. Their most tremendous suffering arises when they declare war on the gods, who are in an even greater position than the demi-gods (a fact the demi-gods refuse to accept). To kill or defeat a god is near impossible as they are stronger and more powerful than the asuras. Whenever there is a fight between them, the gods always win. This kind of situation results in the asuras feeling inferior, then determining to go to war with the gods only to lose over and over again.

The God Realm

This realm is the particular dimension of consciousness and experience that consists of all the five other negative emotions in absolute equality. Diverting pleasure is the fundamental negative emotion of the god realm. The gods are always intoxicated with raw, narcissistic, and distractive pleasures and enjoyments. They live in pure happiness and satisfaction, and they live for long periods. They can live for centuries, millenniums, or even eons. They become so lost in these illusions that they become distracted from the path to enlightenment.

Since all beings' existence depends on the continuity and our perception of karmic experiences, no being can be truly immortal. Unfortunately, lost in their pleasurable lives and incredible longevity, the gods fail to understand this concept, and when the inevitable finally starts to become evident, they begin to suffer. Unable to withstand the truth of their own mortality, the other gods turn away from the dying god, and he/she is left to suffer alone. The condition of the previously flawless body starts to worsen. Besides, the dying gods can see, with their special eyes, the nature of the realm in which they will be reborn to suffer. With this, they begin to experience the sufferings of that particular realm even before they die.

The energy region of divertive pleasure is at the crown of the head. The remedial emotion for their meaningless sense of egocentric satisfaction is empathy and kindness, which comes upon realization of the truth of the mind with the world's real nature.

Why Not Positive Emotions?

Up to this point, all the realms have been said to be based on the experiences of negative karmic emotions. This is not because all those emotions are initially negative in themselves, but because of how we view and react to them. Emotions become negative when we react to them with either attraction or repulsion. However, without emotions, we would not be able to live our lives to the fullest extent. When we let our emotions affect our actions, we open the way for karma to rule and influence our lives. By doing this, we reduce our chance of breaking free from karmic sufferings; we get pushed and pulled in all directions by karma. To avoid this eventual outcome, we will be learning how to expand our sense of conscious awareness and balance it with the inevitable forces of nature.

However, when it comes to emotions, some of our sufferings are spawned from our acts and devices like culture and institutions. We string together situations bound to trigger certain negative emotions, and we suffer from them just the same. These emotions, fear, and depression, for instance, are not widely emphasized in the teachings, yet we experience them in most of our encounters within the samsara. Our only salvation from getting controlled by karma is accepting and understanding the basic fact that everything we do results in encounters of emotional experiences, which are just the illusory protrusion of our minds that we form by allowing ourselves to be overwhelmed with negativities.

In Tibet, we aim at getting emotional freedom. To break free from negative karmic experiences and the emotional sufferings that are related to them. Above all, it is essential to understand that our reaction to a particular emotional experience will make the emotion negative.

Cultivation, Dissipation, and Interaction with Energy Flow

To do all activities in the spiritual world has an energetic basis. In Tibet, this vital energy is known as 'lung.' Still, in the Western part of the world, it is known by its Sanskrit name, 'prana.' The basics of any form of spiritual experience has an energetic basis is to find out why and how something is happening in the form of spiritual experience. We need to identify and recognize the physical and energetic sources to create more experience and successfully segregate the outcomes. This is to determine how to reproduce that same kind of experience and decide whether it is beneficial or harmful to continue the practice.

ENERGY CHANNELS

As for channels, there are various channels for various forms of energetic elements in the body. There are channels for fluids in the body, channels for a more corporeal form of prana, and seemingly endless forms of other media. However, we are concerned with the most basic and unsubstantial form of prana in dream yoga. It is an energy channel that encompasses several forms of subtle energy that we cannot observe in a physical state. We can only prepare ourselves in awareness for them. In our everyday life, we take several postures to make ourselves comfortable per the current situation. When speaking with someone while standing, we may lean against a wall or stand upright to make us feel more relaxed, and when we are about to eat, we sit in a chair to get more comfortable. This same principle is what we follow in assuming different postures in meditation and controlling the other energy channels and their energetic influences on the body. By doing these, we can experience the flow of the different kinds of energy in our bodies. Learning how to control our body's energy points can help us practice the teachings, undergo vital forms of meditation, and sharpen the mind with yoga movements. As an alternative, we could try to use the mind as a primary source of meditation, but at some point, meditation could prove too powerful for the mind. It is better to focus our stream of energy through the six chakras and put it to practice. This would also make it easier for us to overcome the obstacles related to experiencing seamless meditation.

In the study of the energy passages, *prana*, and different chakras in the body, we are concerned with the matter of life as well as death. The strategic movement and channeling of our energetic components guide us in both states of life and death. There has been emphasis regarding the appearance of light and color from people who claim to have had near-death experiences. It is also the Tibetans' belief that these outcomes are a result of *prana* and its channels. We start to experience the decomposition phase of our energy channels' various integral components during the phase of death. From this, some energy is released in the form of lights and color. As we go deeper into the learning of the teachings, we will learn more about how the colored lights are related to different parts of the body and our emotions.

When we die, the colored lights appear to people in different forms, depending on our most prevalent emotions. This is caused by the relationship between our samsaric emotional experiences and the chakras in the body.

Usually, we may experience a simple beam of colored lights with just one primary color at death. We may also experience the collection of lights of several colors, of which one or a few colors are more prevalent than the others. Afterward, the lights may begin to dissolve into shapes, making it look as though we are in a dream. The figures may be of people or things such as houses, palaces, mountains, or virtually any other thing. These images may appear to us as some form of information related to the actuality of samsara. Our reaction to these strings of events will either control us throughout our journey towards our rebirth or manipulate our experiences into conscious meditation, thereby retaining our awareness while positively affecting our next life.

ENERGY PASSAGE

From our several experiences in the samsaric (worldly) field, we have learned that there are different fluids and signal-transporting channels in the human body which travel through various passages. According to anatomical studies, the blood, lymph, waste products, and other body tissues are transported around or out of the body through different channels. However, in addition to these various channels, we have learned of the existence of passages concerned with the dissipation and movement of insubstantial energy forms in dream and sleep yoga. These more superficial forms of energy can either lead us towards embracing negativity or dwelling in absolute wisdom. However, in the corporeal world, these energy points are invisible; we can only feel them in our consciousness.

Inside every person, there are three primary passages in which the six basic chakras are situated. Then, there are three hundred and sixty sub-passages protruding from these direct channels. The sub-passages stretch and extend throughout the entire body. The three main channels are red, white, and blue.

In women, the red passage is situated on the dextral side of the body and the white passage on the sinistral side, while in men, it is vice versa. In both cases, the blue light is situated directly between the other two. The three primary passages unite just below the abdominal region.

The two sideway channels, wide as a small twig, rise all the way up to the brain and turn into a coil just below the roof of the head. They then open out through the nostrils. The blue central channel elongates straight up in-between. It's a bit wider than the other two channels, and from the heart to the crown of the head where it ceases to go further, it widens a little bit more.

The white channel is a means of passage for negative emotions, while the red course is for truth and wisdom. While practicing-dreaming, men sleep with their left side up (to constrict the white channel and open the red channel) while women with their right side up. Doing this helps in dream practice and increasing our chances of cultivating even greater awareness.

The central passage is the tract of monism. It is solely for the circulating of primary awareness. When one practice in dreams, the *prana* is brought into the central channel not to be affected by the other two channels. When we start to experience this, we understand the oneness of the two contrasting dichotomy units.

Karma and Prana

When we act energetically, the karmic forces associated with the results of our actions (either positive or negative) are known as karmic prana. Thus, when the conditions are perfect for manifestation, the karmic traces receive energy and result in the experiences that occur in our mind and body.

The karmic prana controls the mind when the mind is in a state of vulnerability. By reacting to emotions with acknowledgment or severe repulsion, we make our minds susceptible to the influence of negative karmic prana.

In dream practice, it is of utmost vitality to build and improve the state of awareness of our minds to stand on both feet even when we are threatened to get drawn away by negative karmic forces. When practicing dream yoga, we need a considerable surge of spiritual energy to steady and regulate the dream's transparency. We use our internal energy to counteract the continuous channeling of karmic prana and to have considerable leverage over the dream. While still in the preliminary stages, there may be periodic changes when the dream takes control of the dream. This is normal for beginners. As the practice becomes more complex, this will cease to happen.

In Tibetan yoga, we are concerned with three karmic prana forms: bright prana, dark prana, and neutral prana. The bright prana moves through the red channel and is also known as the prana of truth and wisdom. Dark prana controls the flow of negative emotions and is transported through the white channel.

However, the neutral prana is neither of wisdom and truth nor of negative emotions, but yes, it is still karmic in nature. And it spreads out through the entire body. The neutral pranic experiences guide the exponent towards experiencing the prana's immediate nature, which is the non-karmic energy of the blue channel.

PRANIC MOVEMENTS

According to the Tibetan teacher, Long-Chen-pa, there are 21,600 active pranic movements in the body in just one day. With this, we know how tremendous the pranic movements in the body are.

INITIATING PRANIC HARMONY

There is a simple practice for balancing the flow of prana in the body; For men, simply use the left ring finger to block the left nostril, then let out the air with considerable force from the right nostril. As you do this, visualize all your problems and negativities stream out with the air. Afterward, use the right ring finger to block the right nostril and inhale with profound ease with the left nostril. While drawing the air in, think of it flowing in you in the form of pranic wisdom. Keep still and allow the energy to circulate your entire body for a while. Then gently exhale and keep the calm that follows.

As for women, the reverse is the case. Start by using the right ring finger to block the right nostril, then exhale strongly from the left nostril. Then close the left naris with the left ring finger and inhale gently through the right nostril, vividly knowing that you are breathing in the prana of absolute wisdom. Let it flow through your whole body, then exhale with easy gentleness.

Doing this over and over again will help in keeping our internal energy in harmony. We let out all the dark prana through the white passage while letting in the prana of cool wisdom through the red channel, thereby attaining a neutrality state. You should not disturb the calm that follows this process. Rather, you should dwell in it peacefully.

PRANA, MIND AND CHAKRAS

We say that the manifestation of karma in dreams is connected to at least one of the six dimensions, that the relationship is made through certain points in our body. These claims are due to the fact that our physical environment affects our conscious qualities. When we are in a potentially peaceful or beautiful place, for instance, we feel naturally at ease. But when we go to a place where evil has dominated everything else, we feel somewhat nervous or uneasy. That is the state and energy of those places affecting us.

When we concentrate on the visualization of an image or a corporeal object, the quality of the figments and the vividness of our thoughts are based on our meditating environment's spiritual stability and physical state. Furthermore, when we focus our attention on something, it affects our state of mind, and it reflects in the way our body responds. This technique of mental visualization is widely used in healing processes by meditation masters. The focus on a particular object or a phenomenon is utilized in bringing about a change in the body system.

Even in western communities, this method of mental imagery is now being used in the treatment of sicknesses like cancer. According to the Bon tradition, focusing the mind on the conceptual sense of the elements: fire, water, and wind. They believe that the accumulation of negative emotions creates a way for diseases, so instead of determining the nature of diseases, they try to purge the mind of the negative karmic traces, which they believe may be the cause.

Fire, for instance, may be used as a focus object in the treatment of an illness. To do that, try to imagine fiery red triangular images and then creatively feel the heat (as powerful as that of the sun's core) actively flow through your body like surges of infernal hotness. To create more heat, we may have to follow a particular breathing pattern. Like this, we use the images of the mind to influence the body and prana. And it works, despite the fact that we pulled no plug in the physical world. We simply destroy the karmic traces that may be causing us distress. However, for this to work, we must have a rigid sense of purpose as it is not just an expendable process but one that requires an intense understanding of the mind, karma, and internal energy to help in healing. The most critical advantage of this process is that it helps in battling the sole cause of the disease, rather than just the manifestation as well as having no unintended consequences. However, when faced with an illness, it is advisable to use any method that can be advantageous to battle it instead of sticking with only one treatment.

Chakras

Certain points in the body require our concentration during dream yoga. These points are known as chakras, and they are situated at different parts of the body. These chakras are formed by the unity of two or more energy channels. When several channels join one another to connect at a single point, they form an energetic region: a major chakra. From each of these major chakras, several other minor chakras are spawned. We focus our attention on chakras in dream practice.

PART TWO

TYPES AND APPLICATIONS OF DREAMS.

Types of Dreams

In dream practice, we have three types of dreams: Regular samsaric dreams, Transparency dreams, and clear light dreams.

As for the first two types, the main difference is in their source. Also, the practitioner can either be lucid or non-lucid in either case. In clear light dreams, however, we are aware, but we do not participate in the dream with reference to other entities. This type of dream only occurs in a state of non-dual awareness.

Regular samsaric dreams

As stated earlier in the introduction of this book, everybody dreams, and we will continue to dream till we eventually die. Regular samsaric dreams are those that are brought about by the manifestation of karmic traces. Virtually everybody experiences this type of dream. The actuality of this dream is determined by the nature and intensity of the karmic traces that caused it in the first place. These dreams contain meanings, and the meanings are dependent on the state of mind of the dreamer. We can compare the regular samsaric dream to languages. When others speak to us in a language we understand, we sense the meaning almost immediately. When spoken to in a foreign language, however, we do not understand what it is all about. It is the same with dreams. Sometimes, we dream and understand the meaning right away. At other times, we may need to interpret the dreams before we can understand.

Transparency dreams

Dream yoga is a practice that requires great consistency. As we forge deeper into dream yoga, we begin to note more details, remember dreams a lot better than before. This happens as a result of our increased awareness. In dreams of transparency, the prana and the mind are balanced in harmony, and the dreamer is capable of remaining in non-physical consciousness. This type of dream does not drift back and forth like the regular dream. Rather, it abides in intense focus with respect to the dreamer's energy-mind balance. Although there are shapes and experiences in this dream of transparency, they are not caused by karmic forces but by the preoccupation of the dreamer's mind controlled by half-consciousness. This is akin to the difference between the dark karmic prana of the white channel, which is connected with negative emotions, and the truth prana of the red channel. They are both karmic in nature, but one is purer than the other. In the same way, the dream of transparency is also controlled by karmic traces, but it is clearer and purer than the regular samsaric dream.

Transparency dreams are seldom experienced by weak, ordinary minds. They only become a usual experience when our minds have become stable with intense practice. Most people only have samsaric dreams due to the intensity and pressure of the matters in the samsara. Although we may have dreams related to our earlier experience or about the teachings, it may still be a regular dream because it is based on dualism. Therefore, it is advisable to learn about both dreams in detail so as not to make mistakes during practice. To think that samsaric dreams are the dreams that we need to concentrate on can be a total waste of time and effort. Instead, we should note the details and properties of each dream and pay attention to the differences to prevent mistakes.

Clear light dreams

This is an achievement in the spiritual field that comes with great effort and intense practice. It is spawned by the essence of the pristine prana that moves within the central passage. In sleep yoga, teachers have described the clear light as an index of the absolute state of freedom: A state free from dreams, shapes, thoughts, and samsaric disturbances. To attain this level in dream practice is not an easy task. With consistent practice, it may take years or decades to start having clear light dreams.

Trying to achieve this type of dream is like trying to maintain a state of monism during the day. The practitioner must remain in non-dual awareness while blocking out thoughts from perturbing the mind as the presence of thoughts will make one lose focus and slip out of the pure state of rigpa (monism). When we have attained proper stability in rigpa, the thoughts just come and go without any notable hindrance to the practitioner's state of non-dual awareness. This is like trying to do two different tasks at the same time. At first, it seems infeasible, and then as one progresses with consistent practice, it becomes easily doable.

In the dreams of transparency, when we delve into our minds' purest features, we encounter the karmic experiences of less negative emotions, all occurring in a state of duality. This is different in clear light dreams. Here, the dreamer does not observe as a subject with the dream as the corresponding object but proceeds in an intense state of non-dual awareness.

Although the three dreams are different in more extensive aspects, there is the main difference between them: The regular samsaric dream is formed by the karmic traces in the mind of the dreamer, and the dream's dynamism is determined by those traces. In transparency dreams, there is something to be achieved by the dreamer. The karmic traces that form this type of dream are free from the attachment of personal experiences. So, since conscious karma is not entwined, the dreamer can be actively present during the dream and converse with real entities. The knowledge collected in this dream can be of advantage in the samsara.

In clear light dreams, however, there is no dualistic connection between the dream and the dreamer. There is only clear light concentration. Although a dream occurs, the dreamer observes without losing non-dual concentration in the clear light.

Application of Dreams

In our quest for spiritual enlightenment, dreaming is one of the critical factors that shape the nature of our samsaric (worldly) experiences. While we may use dreams as a form of spiritual practice towards attaining increased awareness, we can also use them to: determine our correctness in the process of practicing meditation, make critical decisions regarding our spiritualism, or even use them in deciding if a person is prepared to either start or proceed with practice. In addition, dreams can be used as an indicator to realize when we are lagging while practicing sleep yoga. If we focus intently on our dreams, we will be able to determine which part of our mind is not enlightened. Dreams provide the avenue to work on such part and concentrate our practice where the need be. As the mind becomes greatly pliable when lucid-dreaming, we can do quite a number of things that may be otherwise unfeasible in the physical world. We can develop our mental, emotional and spiritual states in dreams. We can even try to purify our prana (energy flow) and purge ourselves of negative emotions while dreaming. Although beginners can also undergo these practices, it is best to attain absolute lucidity before trying them.

Dreams, Directions, And Divination

When we lucid-dream, we most probably encounter experiences from which we may extract knowledge, meet various beings, or even get warned or instructed about what to do and what to avoid: this is the belief of most spiritual practitioners in Tibet. Furthermore, dreams have been used in determining the state of the body and mind in relation to the different energetic compositions. In Tibet, some people dedicate all their lives to studying dreams and utilizing them in finding solutions to all sorts of spiritual obstacles. Dreams help in the process of diagnosing malignant illness, as well as receiving teachings from spiritual guardians who may appear to certain people in their dreams.

These people consider the guardians as their personal protector. They find meaning to such a dream, apply it in the samsara (world) and pass on the belief to younger practitioners. Sometimes when a guardian appears in a yogi's dreams with a warning, it is said that the warning is to enlighten the yogi of impending danger.

Countless Tibetan yogis who have made great progress in the development of their meditating ability and have become stable in the conscious sense can use the dreams of transparency to either foresee a fragment of what might happen in the future or make certain predictions. This is the basic concept of divination. As stated in the earlier topics, before you can start having dreams of transparency, you must have been capable of breaking free from the karmic traces that usually determine the nature and intensity of the occurrences in dreams, especially in regular samsaric (worldly) dreams, where it is virtually impossible to obtain any useful information. According to the Bon tradition, lucid-dreaming is one of the several techniques used in spiritual divination. This practice is not uncommon in Tibet. Also, students have been said to ask their teachers for instructions regarding the decisions they want to make or about the tasks they want to undergo. In turn, the teachers use their experiences in dreams of transparency to provide solutions for the students.

In a similar manner, we can use the dreams of transparency in satisfying the curiosity of inquisitive minds and finding solutions to the problems of distressed souls.

Divination and the Fluidity of Time

We cannot discuss divination without introducing the concept of time. Some greatly experienced Tibetan masters of meditation receive queries from curious students who think that divination through dreams is tangible proof that the future is constant and not subject to change. According to Tibetan culture, this is wrong. We believe that the future is not fixed. In fact, the future is very much fluid than we can ever imagine. There are vast possibilities of occurrences in the future, and the tools to make them happen are available right now in the present. The sole cost of any experience that is to occur has already been encountered in the past. So, if we have the knowledge of how exactly our actions influence the future, we would be able to control our experiences. This explains the fluidity of time. Because of this, we can change our fate, cure illness, and get protection from going astray. All these would not be possible if the future is fixed. Nothing will be changeable.

Dream As A Teacher

It is possible to receive teachings in a dream. It has happened to many Tibetan practitioners. Most times, reception of these teachings do not occur in a single dream but rather in a string of dreams, with each night's dream being a continuation of the previous nights. The dreams continue each night until the whole message has been relayed. Then the dreams cease. This way, numerous teachings have been learned and passed from generation to generation for centuries. These discoveries are known as gong-ter (mind treasure).

Mind treasures are discovered and learned in the witfulness rather than in the waking state. It is different from entering a hidden space and uncovering a volume of teachings, in which case it is physical. Accomplished Tibetan masters have been said to discover these treasures both in the waking state and while in the dreams of transparency. These treasures are said to be found and learned by meditation masters as it requires advanced practices and enhanced capabilities. Hence, you need to have cultivated the ability to become stable in non-dual awareness without the ordinary self's interference.

The teachings we receive in dreams are not a result of our intelligence or our conceptual understanding. They are like secret treasures we discover when we go on vacation: we did not go on the vacation initially for the treasure. We just came across it by chance. We only use our intellect to make sense of the teachings and store it for future purposes. Aside from the mind treasures, the other sacred teachings were generated from the complexity of human consciousness.

Nevertheless, these forms of teachings can still be similar to one another. If we traced back history to study the different forms of teachings from several times and places, we would still find many resemblances. This is because the teachings were generated by humans when they reached some point in their development of conceptual understanding. The wisdom ingrained in the teachings cannot be confined to one tradition or culture. They can be accessed and understood by any human regardless of their culture or background.

Lastly, the purpose of the teachings that we receive in dreams may vary. The teachings may be for our practice, perhaps as a guideline for enhancing positivity or for the advantage of others.

Uncovering the Bon Practice of Chod

It is possible to make some form of spiritual connection with other people in a different frame of time and space. This window of truth and wisdom has been created in dreams by several yogis who have developed the tremendous ability to enhance their spiritual capabilities. According to the history of the brilliant master of Bon, Tongjung Thuchen, who was believed to have lived in the eighth century, he discovered the practice (a revelatory act of generating kindness and perforating connection) in a sequence of dreams.

Tongjung Thuchen was very young when he started learning about teachings. When he was twelve, he had already attained a high-level development in lucid dreaming. In some of his dreams, he uncovered secret teachings and gained knowledge about the teachings from other spiritual teachers. One day, when he was observing the practice of Walsai, one of the notable deities of Bon, his master called upon him. He discontinued his retreat and traveled to the abode of one of his teacher's patrons. There, he went to sleep and had a wonderful dream.

He saw an attractive woman who led him through strange terrains in his dream, and eventually, they arrived at a graveyard. There were a lot of corpses on the ground. Right at the center of those corpses was a huge white pavilion decorated with beautiful daisies. There stood an enormous throne at the middle of the pavilion, and on that throne sat a brown woman. She was dressed in pure white, and her hair was adorned with turquoise and gold ornament. Several pretty dakinis (spiritual beings in female form) were assembled around her, conversing in different languages. From this, Tongjung Thuchen could tell that they were from far away countries.

The brown woman stood and approached Tongjung Thuchen with a human skull filled with blood and flesh and gave him to eat and drink from it. Then, she told him that these were his offerings and that he should accept it unsullied distinction. She also told him that she, together with the other dakinis, was going to initiate him.

She then said to him, "You shall attain enlightenment in the space of the Great Mother. I am Sippe Gyalmo, the guardian of the Bon teaching, the Brown Queen of Existence. This initiation and teaching is the archetypal root of Mother Tantra. You are initiated to teach and initiate others." She then led him to a magnificent throne. He was given a ceremonial hat, an initiation cloak, and some tools for performing sacred rituals. Sippe Gyalmo then asked him to initiate the assembled dakinis.

Tongjung Thuchen was very surprised at this. He then tried to protest by claiming that he did not know how to perform initiation. "This is very embarrassing," he said.

Sippe Gyalmo restored his confidence by reassuring him that he was an accomplished master of spiritualism and that he could perform the initiation.

"I don't know what or how to sing during the rituals," he objected.

Then Sippe Gyalmo said, "The masters empower you, and you have my help. Do not be afraid. Please commence the initiation."

At that very moment, there was a mass transformation of the items in the tent. All flesh and blood had disappeared, and its place was several food items and flowers and medicines. Then, he saw himself being sprayed with flowers by the dakinis. All of a sudden, he became aware of his ability to perform the initiation ritual for the Mother Tantra, and he immediately performed it.

All of the dakinis appreciated him afterward. Then Sippe Gyalmo said to him, "Five years from now, the dakinis from the eight most significant graveyard will meet, as will numerous masters. If you come, you would receive more teachings from the Mother Tantra." Afterward, all the dakinis bid him goodbye, and he did the same. Then Sippe Gyalmo told him it was time for him to leave. A red Dakini stepped forward, took a scarf, and wrote a symbol representing the power of the wind element on it. She then waved the scarf in the air and requested that he touch the scarf using his right foot. As he did so, he was back in his body, sleeping in full awareness.

He was asleep for so long that people supposed that he was dead. He later awoke and narrated his experience to his teacher, who found it amazing. His teacher then warned him to keep it secret to avoid obstacles. Tougjung Thuchen then received his teacher's blessing, which would help him relay his teachings effectively in the future.

After the year, Tougjung Thuchen was in deep meditation when three dakinis visited him. They had green scarves which they used to touch his feet. As soon as they did so, he fell asleep and woke in a dream.

Three caves were facing the east direction. He also saw there was a magnificent body of water just in front of the caves. He then strolled through and found himself in the middle cave. There were three masters in the cave, which was beautified with adorable flowers. Each of the masters was dressed in an initiation cloak, all with different patterns. There were several charming dakinis assembled around them, doing all sorts of spiritual processions.

The three masters then initiated Tougjung Thuchen, thereby awakening his primordial sense. He could then remember his past lives and teach the Bon practices without difficulty. The master sitting in the middle then rose and said, "You have received all the sacred teachings. You are initiated and gotten our blessings so that you can teach others."

The master who was sitting to the right also rose and said, "You are empowered with all the general teaching; how to allow emotions to self-liberate with conceptual mind and the use of logical discipline to destroy the ego. We have given our blessing, and you shall continue to practice and teach the practices to others."

Then the master who sat to the left rose and said, "You are about to receive the sacred art of Tantric teaching that occupy the space in the heart of all Tibetan and Zhang Zhung masters. You shall use the knowledge which you have attained to help others."

These three masters had lived over five hundred years before Tougjung Thuchen was born in the eighth century, yet he was still able to receive teachings from them. Such is the uniqueness and importance of the Bon practice.

He continued to receive sacred teachings by various masters in his dreams. He had achieved the capability to be present and aware in dreams and relate with energetic forms of spiritual beings. On several occasions, he walked without his feet touching the ground, and he could move very, very swiftly through space with the help of his energetic core (prana).

After four years, the time for Tongjung Thunchen's meeting with the spiritual masters and dakinis had come, according to what the brown Dakini (the embodiment of Sippe Gyalmo) had told him. On this fateful day, he woke up after a quick prayer nap and found that the sky was extraordinarily clear. He felt the breeze blow, and suddenly, two dakinis who rode the wind appeared to him; they told him that they had come to take him. He left with them, and they arrived at a space with a large assembly of dakinis. He recognized them as the dakinis from five years earlier. He was then taught all the breakdown and complete illustrations of the sacred practices of chod and the Mother Tantra. He even experienced a prophecy made by the dakinis: that there would be a time in the future when mahasattvas and twelve masters who had received blessings would emerge and that Tongjung Thuchen would also be privileged to teach at the same period. Following this, each of the dakinis promised to help him in the course of his teaching. Sippe Gyalmo, the brown Dakini, also made a vow to help focus his teachings and protect them from negative apprehension. One by one, all the dakinis made promises to help with the dispersion of the teachings. They also told him that the dispersion of the teachings would take place in ten directions, just like the rays of sunlight, till it circulates the whole world.

The illustration of this man's life is a perfect instance regarding the dreams of transparency. He met with beings of energetic basis in his dreams and witnessed accurate instructions and prophecies. Even the fact that he was a master was unknown to him until it was revealed to him in his dreams. He did not stop receiving teachings, developing through his conventional self, and meeting great teachers and dakinis throughout his life.

We can do it, too. We have now experienced the proof that dreams are very critical in the practice of spiritualism. We need to undergo deep and consistent practice in dreams to help quicken the development of our true selves.

PART THREE

THE YOGA OF DREAMS IN PRACTICAL SENSE

Perception, Behavior, Dream, And

Death

According to the Mother Tantra, the way one perceives any experience will determine one's behavior and response towards that particular experience. It is vital to stay conscious of behavior as it is the starting point for developing one's awareness when in dreams and the state after death.

When we are not really aware of our true self and existence, it becomes burdensome to correspond with the samsaric. We are just dependent on the flow of karmic traces that toss us here and there, without any sense of enlightenment.

As explained in previous chapters, the waking days are created by the manifestation of several karmic traces, and so does it happen in dreams as well. If we are not able to reach beyond the grasp of karma and the samsaric delusions during the day, we would definitely be unable to escape the karmic obstacles in dreams. If we refused to be enlightened, the phenomena we experience in dreams would affect us in the same way the negative emotions do during the day. We will most likely respond in a dualistic manner.

When we die, our experiences upon entering the bardo (the intermediate state after death) depends on the entirety of our habitual activities, including the way we respond to Karmic manifestations. The whole process of experiencing the bardo is similar to falling asleep. With a mind that has not been sharpened for enhanced awareness, we just slip into a state controlled by the forces of Karmic traces. Once more, we would experience several occurrences that all segregate from karma, and then, death too would be without meaning and purpose.

On the other hand, when we cultivate the sense of habitual consciousness and apply it to each of our primordial experiences, we will steadily enhance our awareness and stay conscious in dreams. Then, as we undergo incessant dream practice, our awareness becomes greatly developed, and by doing that, we say that we are preparing for the intermediate state after death. This is one of the main reasons for consistent dream practice: we are not controlled by karmic manifestation in dreams and after death.

However, to attain development in dream practice, there are obstacles we need to overcome. The first is training the mind to become stable and vivid to preserve awareness in every experience we encounter. As we progress, it becomes relatively easier to respond to experiences with absolute positivity. Then, we say that we have attained "awareness in behavior."

Usually, by cultivating awareness in our behavior, the resultant change in our response to karmic experiences begins to manifest in dreams. As we continue to bring awareness into dreams by observing the state of non-dualistic responses during the day, we are getting our minds prepared to undergo the four basic practices on the path to enlightenment. When done consistently, these practices enable us to learn how to further stretch our flexible mind beyond the boundaries of samsaric constrictions. We do this by using every objective encounter we experience during the day as a point of focus to enhance lucidity and prevent the emergence of karmic traces.

In dream yoga, there are preliminary practices that you can perform to cultivate a greater sense of consciousness. In these practices, we use the knowledge of prana, energy point, and the mind to achieve and maintain absolute lucidity in dreams. In Tibet, these primary practices are observed at night before going to sleep and during the three waking hours of the night. Once we have achieved greater awareness with these practices, there are more advanced practices that we need to undergo so as to finally pierce through the constraining boundaries and the delusions of the samsara in which we have been trapped.

Our stability and level of dualism in the state of the bardo are dependent on how lucidity in a dream. It follows that our level of awareness during the waking hour of the day will affect how clear and lucid our dream practice will be.

Similarly, our dreams' lucidity will affect our transparency and our ability to make conscious choices while influencing the stability of the other states. That is why it is important to pay attention to the subtlest of the practices as we work our way out of samsaric limitations.

The Art of Calm Abiding (Zhine)

Even after attaining lucidity in dream yoga, it is vital to maintain the state of regulated awareness. The process of maintaining the mind's stability manifests in the dreams. You start to experience more clarity in your dreams, you begin to dream for longer periods, and you remember the details more easily. This is not all. You also experience more clarity in the samsara. It becomes easier to live without getting blown off by karmic negativities that would otherwise determine and shape all your experiences, not only in the waking state but also in dreams.

In sleep and sleep yoga, as well as other spiritual spheres, certain practices are performed to help unite and focus the mind on deepening meditation. In Tibet, these practices are known as Zhine (calm abiding), and there are three levels according to how stable one's practice is:

Forcible Zhine, Natural Zhine, and Final Zhine. In the practices of Zhine, we start by projecting mental focus upon an object. However, as time goes on, when we have developed strong concentration levels, we begin to practice without the use of an object.

First, clear your mind of lingering samsaric negativities, let go of negative emotions, and then sit with your legs crossed. Place one hand on top of the other such that the back of the palm of one hand rests on the palm of the other and position them both on the upper region of your laps. Your spine should be straight but not rigid. Slant your head down a little to align the neck with the spine, and your eyes must be open. The muscles in your eyes should be relaxed. Do not squint or widen your eyes. The object of central focus should be positioned in a way that allows you to look straight ahead at it without disrupting the sitting posture you have maintained. Then, try to focus without moving. Keep still and continue to breathe naturally.

Usually, although we can use anything when practicing with an object, it is advisable to use the Tibetan letter "A" as the object of focus.

There are many meanings related to the letter's emblematic nature, but its purpose here is to help build our power of concentration. Other objects that may be used include the English letter "A," a lucky charm, or even the sound of breaths. We can use virtually anything, but it is preferable to use something that we consider sacred so that we can get inspiration from it. Plus, it is advisable to use the same object every time rather than selecting a different object each time. This is to avoid a situation of focus deflection when we are already underway.

Assuming you are using the Tibetan "A," write it on a not-too-thin piece of paper of around one-inch square. Then glue the paper to a wall or stick that is high enough for you to view at eye level in the five-point sitting position explained earlier. If you are using a stick, make sure it is rigid and not shaking. Position it such that the distance between your eyes and the paper is between one to two feet.

As you develop in this practice, the power and strength of your focus greatly improve, and you begin to meditate for much longer. When this happens, you may start to experience the perception of strange feelings in your body. You start visualizing strange events within your mind. All these are normal; they are just signs that your body is positively responding to the practice. So, it is pointless to develop too much interest in them.

FORCIBLE ZHINE

The term "forcible" was used to describe this focus development stage because it calls for a great effort. It is not easy to sharpen an ordinary mind with the arts of intense concentration, but we will find the solution here. For a mind that has been dominated by the affairs of the samsara for so long, it would seem cumbersome at first. Distraction will come and go as easily as blinking an eye, and it may seem like an insurmountable task to concentrate on a single object by blocking out all thoughts for a minute.

At first, when it all seems difficult, it is advisable to practice in several brief periods with short breaks in-between. During the breaks, do not think of any other things or allow the samsaric illusions to occupy your mind. Rather, you can visualize objects mentally to enhance your concentration power further or perform other practices like the generation and development of positive emotions. Then, when it is time to return to practice, do so without any hesitation. However, if you intend to practice, there is no means of getting your object of focus, simply imagining a sphere of light just above your glabella, right on your forehead. Try to focus on that sphere of light without allowing your mind to roam away. Doing this once or twice daily is accepted, but it is recommended to do it more frequently if there is time. This practice involves expanding our mental capability, and it is similar to bodily exercise that we do to strengthen our muscles. Thus, we must practice from time to time. While practicing, all the extensions of your mind should be based on the object of focus. It is pointless to practice with the mind dwelling on the issues of the past or the expectations of the future. No form of disturbance should distract you, so it is advisable to use a silent place. Do not lose sight of the object. Concentrate on it with all your might and transparency. You are connecting your mind with the object using your eye as the only channel, in the case of visual focus. Keep your awareness of that object at all times. Let your breathing be very steady and keep it gentle till your breathing blends with the environment, and you lose the sense of breathing. Then gradually, let the calm and quiet rise within and around you. But be sure your body is not all strained up in focus; allow your body to relax. This does not mean that you should let your body become dazed or fall into a trance. More importantly, it is useless to let your thought wander around the object. That is to say; you should not think about the object or the circumstances surrounding it. Instead, remain conscious of its presence. To think of the object is not what this practice is all about. As a beginner, you face the possibility that your attention will get diverted. When it does, calmly bring it back to the object and let it remain there.

NATURAL ZHINE

As you attain progress, you reach the natural zhine: the second phase of practice. In the first phase, it was all about forcing the mind to focus on an object by consistently diverting our attention from other things and concentrating on a sole particle. Here, the mind will already have gotten used to the object's presence and will concentrate on it with little effort. There is an establishment of agreement in which the thought originates without affecting our attention to the object. Our physical component gets united, and the energy channel directs the prana without any difficulty. At this point, we become fit to focus in the absence of an object.

In place of the object of focus, simply direct your attention towards the infinite space. You can either gaze into an open space or practice inside a small room by focusing on the emptiness between yourself and the wall. Abide in gentle calmness and relax your body. During this practice, it is helpful to allow the mind to expand and thin out, rather than just concentrating on a visualized position in space. When the mind spreads out in space, we say that we are blending the mind with nothingness. Doing this gets us prepared for the third and final phase of the Zhine practice.

FINAL ZHINE

This is the phase where the cultivation of calmness and lightness is ultimate. To get to this stage, one must have been able to focus with or without an object directly. In the previous phases, the practitioner still experiences some difficulties in maintaining the clarity of the mind. But in this phase, there is total and absolute transparency. Although there are certain distractive thoughts, they vanish on their own without any effort applied. Thoughts just arise and disperse without any difficulty.

During this stage, there is a tradition in the Dzogchen culture in which the teacher allows the student to learn the art of attaining the natural state of mind. In this culture, it is believed that this practice for the student to know the distinction between the ever-changing mind and the mind blessed with ultimate monism (rigpa).

HINDRANCES

To make significant progress in these arts of Zhine, there are certain impediments that we need to watch out for. The first is encountered when the mind becomes restless and anxious. In this state, we experience incessant streams of thoughts, making it difficult to settle one's concentration on a particular thing. To avoid this, we should away from physical, mental, and emotional stress before practice. We may also try some yogi stretches while simultaneously making mental attempts to calm the body and mind. Afterward, do some breathing exercises to prepare your mind for practice. Immediately you commence, do not let any thought distract you from preventing the mind's attention from getting diverted while maintaining the five-point sitting posture.

The second obstacle to be overcome is sleepy dullness. This is the hindrance that impedes one's ability to refine consciousness. The dullness occurs due to foggy boredom that prevents the mind from concentrating on the object. When this happens, you can either try to apply more effort into concentration to pierce through the drowsiness, or you can take a break, recite some mantras and do some stretching exercise.

The third hindrance that most yogis encounter is slackness. A deceptive feeling of lazy calmness characterizes this hindrance. This is a state when you feel relaxed but with a negligible sense of concentration. It would be best if you were very careful during practice not to get trapped by this obstacle. One may mistake this state for the actual meditation state, thus wasting a lot of time doing the wrong practice without attaining any form of mental awareness. When your attention becomes slackened and you start to lose concentration, quickly re-align your posture and strengthen your focus on the object. While you proceed with this practice, try to bear in mind that you are performing the sacred practices of attaining enlightenment, which is the realization of the mind that many people crave. This should serve to inspire you to keep going. Also, try to realize the purpose of your intentions, and it will help to empower the consciousness of your mind regarding the practice.

As stated earlier, it is important to practice the zhine as frequently as humanly possible as it is not only to prepare us for further practices but also to maintain mental stability at any point in our lives. It would not be ideal to abandon the practice after we have supposedly attained stability. The practice is meant for continuous observation for regulating the mind's awareness. When we consistently strengthen ourselves in the conscious sense, it becomes apparent in dreams, and we ultimately become prepared for advances yogic practices.

The Four Basic Yogic Practices

These are the practices that are commonly referred to as preparatory practices. This does not mean that we should practice them with frivolity. They are just as important as the other practices that follow, and to perform them successfully will further increase your chance of attaining success in the following practices.

Basically, to practice dream yoga, you allow your mind to explore the space and the sense of enlightenment hidden beyond the samsara's delusions. To achieve that, you need to undergo the four preparatory yogic practices and succeed. The shape and nature of our experiences during the waking state and dreams are all determined by the way we use our minds. These practices are centered on changing the way we view the objects and experiences of the samsara and subsequently changing the shape and quality of our dreams. The two concepts are mutually interrelated. Your most dominant emotions and experience during your activities in the samsara is the one that will most likely manifest in your dreams. Similarly, if you start cultivating more intense awareness in the waking state, you will undoubtedly experience that increased awareness in dreams.

First Basic Practice: Realization

This practice is centered on changing the karmic traces that affect our experiences when we are awake as well as when we are in dreams. The first step is to abandon the samsaric knowledge and face the ultimate reality that the waking state is just another form of a dream. If you do not understand this fact, it would be difficult to undergo any basic practices. Simply try to base all your encounters in the samsara with your developing realization that you are in a dream. Upon waking from sleep, maintain the realization that 'you are awake in a dream.' Regard everything you do and encounter as the affairs of the dream you are experiencing.

When you shower in the morning, think of the water flowing down your body as dream water. Do this for every other thing you do experience the whole day. Keep reminding yourself of that realization continuously to keep your mind aware.

However, this realization should only manifest in you, the dreamer, rather than the objects and experiences of the dream. Everything you feel should also be considered as part of the dream. The surge of energy or splash of drowsiness you feel in the morning, the anger you feel when your neighbor next door infuriates you, the excitement you feel when you go on vacation - they are all in the dream. Knowing and accepting this fact allows the mind to earnestly start to believe that all our experiences are just the manifestation of karmic traces and that these experiences are as tenuous as our encounters in the dream. By considering all the samsaric occurrences as insubstantial, our dualistic response towards them becomes negligible. That is to say, our reactions of acknowledgment and repulsion decrease. Following this, the dream-world realization also becomes habitual, manifesting in every one of our experiences in the waking state, as well as in dreams.

In this particular practice, we can either consider the realization that we are in a dream as a way of changing karmic traces and subsequently, changing the way we relate to the samsaric affairs, or think of it as a method of acknowledging the nothingness of the world, that everything we do and experience is all the delusions of our mind, powered by the samsara. Either way, we should be focused on the aim of attaining the primary realization.

Another way of making this practice easier is by thinking of yourself as an illusory being, in a feeble body with the knowledge of space and time. Accept it and let the surge of realization overwhelm you. This is what the first practice is all about: to see everything for what they are, a dream. However, the approach of realizing that the world is insubstantial and without essence should not prevent us from taking adequate measures to abide by the rules and precepts of the samsara. It would be illogical to think that since the world is like a dream, we should be able to do extraordinary things like riding above the clouds or acting without consequence. While retaining the realization that occurrences in dreams are as actual as our waking experiences, we should also try to be aware of the world's limitations. For example, if you cut yourself, you will bleed out, and if you bang your head against the wall, you will get hurt. This is a world governed by karmic forces, where every action has a corresponding consequence. Our goal is to attain freedom and enlightenment to expand our minds further to accommodate truth and absolute wisdom. With this, we can penetrate the karmic boundaries restraining us to our conventional selves.

Second Basic practice: Banishing Dualism

The second fundamental practice involves learning to prevent the mind from dwelling on the world's dualistic features. This second practice is not so different from the first. The primary difference is that it was all about attaining realization within the mind without performing any physical activity in the first practice. In contrast, the second preparation is based on training the mind to decrease its dualistic response towards resultant karmic experiences. The first practice allows us to achieve greater awareness and clarity in our experiences, both in the dream and waking states. We aim to attain in the second preparatory practice awareness of the way we react to karmic experiences. Either way, the decrement of karmic traces is of utmost importance.

Acknowledgment and repulsion may arise from any reaction in the form of emotions like pleasure, anger, joy, expectation, depression, sadness, disappointment, envy, or other negative emotions.

To banish these emotions from the mind, you must first realize that the whole thing is a dream. Then absorb the truth in that realization and let it consume you. Doing this, you recognize yourself as the sole cause of the anger you feel, the sadness and disappointment you are drowning in. It was all initiated from inside you through a complicated interaction of several internal activities. Upon becoming aware of this fact, it becomes clear that all forms of emotions are just made up of our conventional mind's conceptual fantasies.

Essentially, as humans, there are vast measures of occurrences to which we tend to react. This makes us very prone to reacting to events in a dualistic manner. Therefore, we should learn to imprint the realization of the world's dream-like nature not just in our thoughts but also in our buildup of experience and, ultimately, our feelings. Dualism is a state characterized by karmic bondage, and it is not until we understand this that we will attain enlightenment. When we undergo the foundational practices with profound consistency and diligence, it becomes relatively easy to counteract our impulsive preoccupation with the samsara. Our irrational affinity for negative emotions causes this unhealthy fixation on the samsara. Being able to effectively employ the potentially efficient practices to dissolve negative karmic emotions is denotive that we are genuinely prepared for the awareness and clarity required for a smooth course in sleep and dream yoga. One usually starts by dealing with emotions of faint intensity. But with regular and consistent practice, we begin to take on stronger intensity emotions even without realizing it.

One of a brilliant practitioner's qualities is the ability to do practices as specified in the teachings. In this practice, for instance, there are other not-so-healthy ways to prevent the manifestation of negative emotions. Instead of utilizing the wisdom in the teachings, some people decide to bottle up emotions and feelings inside themselves. This way, it becomes a hindrance to attaining spiritual progress and also a cause for inner distress and anguish. Rather than trying to escape our experiences' torments, it would be of more significant advantage to becoming a monial or an anchorite.

In sleep and dream yoga, we attain freedom and escape the clutches of karmic manifestations by revising and decentralizing our perception of the world's totality. This way, we are not carried away by the illusions of the objects and situations that arise as a form of karmic manifestations. Continuous practice helps consider items and experiences as ephemeral and immaterial. We attain peacefulness and freedom by decreasing the mind's dualistic nature rather than trying to flee undesirable situations through suppression and ignorance.

Third Basic Practice: Empowering Purpose

The first and second practices encompass the art of diminishing karmic manifestations during the day by learning to decrease our levels of dualistic responses: Acknowledgement and repulsion. However, the third practice is concerned with revising the experiences of the day right before going to sleep. Just before you fall asleep, gently try to remember the various activities of the day.

As the memories start to flow into your mind, maintain the realization that you retain a dream. At that moment, the experiences you remember are the ones that are most likely to manifest in your upcoming dreams because there is little difference between memories and dreams. Once more, the process of acknowledging your recollections as a dream should not be just a repetitive practice of thoughts with a single statement. We should feel the difference internally and begin to appreciate the sense of peacefulness that succeeds it.

Afterward, acquire the purpose of acknowledging the nights' dreams as they are. Then develop a firm intention of realizing with clarity, in dreams, that you are dreaming. This will allow you to create greater awareness and feel a more substantial presence of yourself in dreams. As for the development of intentions, the phrase "making a wish" is the English translation of a Tibetan saying, used to expound the process, making it easier for practitioners. According to the saying, the generation of purpose can be related to making a wish or sending requests to the energetic form of beings, deities, or masters. Amongst several other practices that can be performed before going to sleep, this one is the easiest and requires fewer resources.

Fourth Basic practice: Strengthening the memory

We begin the fourth fundamental practice when we wake in the morning. Start by slowly taking notes of the night's events. Try to remember if you dreamed. Then determine the nature of your dream. Remember if your dream was lucid, that is, if you were aware of yourself in the dream. Do not rush the memories. Calmly take note of the details as they start to resurface. That is what the fourth primary practice is all about: developing a greater purpose and stronger memory to remember dreams better. However, when we dream but find it difficult to remember the dream, we should make a resolution to cultivate a greater sense of purpose and intention to make progress when going to sleep the next night. Afterward, suppose you still encounter difficulties remembering dreams. In that case, it is recommended to practice the art of developing and maintaining a strong sense of purpose throughout the day, and when it is time to sleep at night, express the desire and intention of remaining lucid in your dreams vividly in your thoughts.

If you attained clarity in your dreams during the night, you have achieved an excellent task. Rejoice at the achievement. Then, maintain the intention to perform better the next night. Keep repeating the process, using each night's dream lucidity as an avenue to make a resolution towards attaining greater purposes and better performances. Recognize even your resolution as a dream.

Lastly, upon awakening in the morning, make it your priority to practice the whole day and develop the purpose to maintain consistency in practice. It is also recommended to make a prayer at this moment. Pray for accomplishment; pray not to encounter obstacles.

This last practice combines with the first, the realization practice. This way, these practices become normalized; we go on with it while blending it with our samsaric affairs.

Additional Note

These four foundational practices are so critical to the practitioner's progress in other spiritual practices. Practicing them is necessary to move on to the more complicated phases of dream and sleep yoga. They are very advantageous and pose less difficulty than other practices. Practicing for a day or two, then stopping may come out as a futile effort. Thus, it is very vital to remain consistent until absolute clarity is attained. Regularly doing these practices makes it possible for us to cultivate a more significant presence during the day. Even when the reality is lost, it will be attained back without notable effort. Asides from acquiring increased transparency and spiritual awareness, these practices are also advantageous when undergoing the samsaric affair. The mind becomes sharpened and empowered with the state of active presence. The practitioner's memory also becomes enhanced as he/she gradually attains lucidity.

Furthermore, it is pointless to abandon the practice because you are not experiencing any results. Life is a gradual process; nothing stays the same forever. When you practice without attaining lucidity, apply more effort to the practice, reflect on your experimental procedures, and determine if you have made an error. In either case, it is ideal to consider it as an obstacle that you need to overcome.

How to Prepare For The Night

At night, an ordinary person, without any knowledge of the teachings, goes to bed with a burdened mind. A mind that had been weighed down with the worries and emotions of the waking hours. There is no resolution to practice or cultivate any form of awareness or clarity. Then sleep arises amidst the several negative karmic emotions that had been imprinted upon the mind while experiencing the samsara's waking hours. During sleep, such a mind will be torn between the appearance of imminent dreams and the unstable karmic traces that keep influencing it. These adversely affect the physical body as well as the body's pranic activities. The body becomes overwhelmed with spiritual fatigue, and when the sleeper wakes up, they mostly carry the previous day's negativities into the new day's experiences. This is immensely harmful to our spiritual health. Even if we have no interest in the dream and sleep yogic activities, it would still be advantageous to make specific preparations before we sleep: attaining freedom from the day's negative emotions and purging the mind of the lingering karmic traces by utilizing any form of meditative knowledge we possess. In sleep and dream yoga, it is of utmost importance that we get a peaceful sleep. Liberating the mind of karmic forces before rest has many benefits, of which an increased chance for attaining lucidity is one. The importance of these preparatory practices cannot be overemphasized. So, even if we cannot observe every one of the practices, we should make sure to clear the mind of all negativities before sleep.

A night free of trouble is always characterized by the absence of karmic traces and negative emotions. We can undergo numerous forms of practices at night while preparing for peacefulness and lucidity in sleep and dream. Some of the fundamental techniques required to purify the mind and cultivate presence during sleep are listed below:

THE MIND CLEANSING BREATHING

It is not uncommon to experience how different situations affect our breathing patterns. Whether we are either tensed or relaxed, it is always evident in our body's reaction, especially how we live through and react to situations. In the previous chapters, we had discussed the different ways of achieving awareness to help in our response to various samsaric experiences. Now it is time to learn how to utilize our breathing pattern to enhance practice and attain more excellent results. Our breathing pattern is mostly denotive of the experience we are passing through at a point in time. For instance, when you are alone with someone you truly love, your breathing slows down, your pupils dilate, and your body muscles relax all together.

On the other hand, when you get chased by a dog, you become overcome by fear, and the immediate need to get away becomes your priority. During that brief period, you will probably experience fast breathing, consisting of short and very sharp breaths. This explains how different situations and experiences alter our breathing patterns. Taking advantage of this principle, this practice is based on experiencing the conditions the other way round. That is, instead of allowing experiences to determine the way we breathe, we can knowingly modify our breathing pattern to adapt to our experiences. This particular practice is a brief breathing exercise consisting of nine unique breaths. With this practice, we can cleanse the mind, clear our energy channels and smoothen the prana.

To begin, clear your mind of all thoughts. Take the five-point sitting posture: sit down with your legs crossed, place your left hand on your right with both palms facing up. Then, align your neck with the spine by bending down your head a little.

Imagine the three main pranic passages in the body. In your mind's eye, visualize the blue central channel, like a small pipe, as it elongates centrally upwards in the body. The two other passages, one on either side of the main channel, merge at the central passage base just some inches below the abdomen. Then they rise upwards to the skull, where they form some twist. They continue to elongate past the central channel, which stops at the head. Then they open at the nares.

FIRST STEP

For women

Press your left thumb against the root of your left fourth finger and hold it there. Then use your left fourth finger to block the left naris.

Visualize the air as green in color and draw in the green air with the right naris. Then plug the right naris with the right fourth finger and breathe out the light blue air through the left naris. Do this three times.

For men

Press your right thumb to the root of the right fourth finger and block your right naris with the right fourth finger. Then draw in the green air through the left naris. Afterward, close the left naris with the left ring finger and let out the air through the right naris.

While expelling each breath, envisage yourself letting out all hindrances associated with the male essence through the white channel. Those hindrances may be problems related to one's past or even illnesses pertaining to wind energy.

SECOND STEP

The processes of this step are the same for both men and women. Repeat the first step, but in this case, use the right ring finger to block the left nostril and vice versa. As you expel the light pink air, envisage all hindrances associated with the female essence come out with the air.

Examples of these hindrances are sicknesses related to gall and impediments of the future.

THIRD STEP

This practical step is also the same for men and women. Return to the five-point sitting posture with your hands positioned correctly on your laps. Then inhale the green air with both nostrils open. As you do so, envisage green light traveling through both the side energy passages down your body. Focus your mind's eye as you visualize the green light from each side passage merges with the central course below the navel. Then, see it within yourself as the energy rises through the central pranic passage and as it opens at the top of the head. Do this three times also. As you expel air each time, envisage all forms of hindrances associated with evil spirits' essence exit from your head in the form of black vapor. Examples of these are sicknesses related to viscid mucus and problems and impediments of the present.

The Ultimate Practice Of 'Guru Yoga'

The term 'guru' is used for describing a Master that is spiritually accomplished and is completely qualified as a teacher. The Master is not an actual being but the summation of all the teachings we have received. This also includes the teachers from whom we have learned. This practice involves getting connected with The Master. In the process of being consistent with the attainment of enlightenment, it becomes an irremovable part of us. We get immensely attached to the firm root of the practice. The sole aim of 'guru yoga' is to blend the student's mind with that of The Master.

The Master is the fluid, primordial nature of the mind. The essence of one's awareness and the amorphous root upon which everything else is placed. The true Master is without a particular shape, but we have to envisage it in a form due to our dualistic nature. This is an advantage to us beings of dualistic minds. This practice lets us utilize dualism to attain enlightenment and develop our ability to make conscious, more positive choices.

In this practice, the envisioning of deities is variable depending on your tradition or lineage. While some practitioners may choose to visualize gods like Tapihritza, Buddha Shenlha Odka, others may decide to use the forms of other notable deities as their Master form. However, it is vital to choose a being that you know about because envisioning The Master is incorporating all the teachers with whom you have practiced, all the generative teachings you have received, and the ultimate progression of your primeval monism.

The masters and deities that once lived were successful in discovering their primal state of mind and lived in absolute enlightenment. That is what we aim to achieve with this practice. To practice 'guru yoga' is to cultivate immense commitment towards your primordial mind; to exhibit great love for the envisioned deity and the 'guru' itself. This is because the primal state of mind is your entirely qualified teacher and real confidant.

The Practice

Following the nine breaths practice observation, maintain the five-point sitting position correctly, and envisage The Master overhead you and before you. The visualized image should not be flat or without sensible detail. The picture you are envisioning should be as stereoscopic as possible, with light radiating off every inch and with an existence that influences the way you feel at that moment. Let the being of The Master rush through you in waves of awareness. Then allow the understanding to control your pranic components, as well as your mind. There, develop a stable sense of fidelity and faithfulness towards The Master and appreciate them for the tremendous volume of teachings you have been privileged to obtain. Afterward, pray to The Master that you succeed in developing a mind of positivity, that you encounter fewer negative energies, and that you achieve success in sleep and dream yoga.

Then envision yourself getting The Master's blessings. Imagine these blessings in the form of lights, beaming from The Master's three passages of truth and wisdom, into yours. The three passages are of the body, speech, and mind. Imagine white light beaming from the brow chakra of The Master into yours, cleansing and filling your body with calmness. Then imagine red light surging from The Master's throat chakra into yours, cleansing and smoothening your energetic composition. Lastly, imagine the blue light flowing from The Master's heart chakra into yours, and feel it cleansing and putting your mind at ease.

As you imagine, be aware of these lights enter your body, feel their presence and influence in your body. Allow your mind to accommodate the wisdom and truth that this practice provides. Keep imagining yourself utilizing these blessings in vivid experiences and receiving inspiration from them. Make these positive energies easily accessible in your body, experiences, and mind. Then visualize The Master melting into the light and imagine that light entering your heart, never to leave again. Feel your core getting empowered with calm. Abide in that calm and dissolve your mind in the non-dualistic state of monism (rigpa).

There are more intricate forms of the 'guru yoga' practice. These may involve envisioning more challenging positions and making extensive offerings, but the instructions' primary root is to dissolve one's mind with The Master's. This allows us to abide in the state of absolute monism.

We can do the 'guru yoga' practice at any time of the day, and it can be done as frequently as possible. But the more we do it, the better. This practice is so vital to attaining enlightenment. It allows one to receive blessings from The Master and soften the hardened mind towards achieving enlightenment.

The Principal Practices in Dream Yoga

There are certain practices that we need to go through to be successful in dream yogi. It is necessary to undergo these practices in a sequential form:

- Accommodating presence in the central passage
- Developing transparency
- Becoming stronger to avoid getting lost
- Overcoming fear

The wisdom embedded within these instructions is the primary goal of the general practice of dream and sleep.

ACCOMODATING PRESENCE IN THE CENTRAL PASSAGE

Before commencing these practices, you must have gone through the waking hours' preparatory exercises, the practices before going to sleep (nine cleansing breathing), the guru yoga, and the resolution for the night's practice.

Begin by lying down on your side. Men should lie with their left side facing up, and vice versa in women. Then bend your legs so that your knees are almost at the same level as your lower abdomen. Align the arm on the upper side with the body length. The other arm should be positioned comfortably under the cheek. This sleeping position is called the lion posture. Then calm yourself so that your breaths may be gentle and relaxed. Do not let the sound of your breathing manifest: keep it as quiet as you can.

Envisage the presence of a red lotus at the base of the throat, exactly where the throat chakra is located. Observe, with your mind, the upright lotus at the throat chakra and adore its four beautiful petals. Just at the center of the four petals is the Tibetan letter 'A,' which radiates a reddish light from its smooth, luminous surface.

The reddish glow is a result of the white light that the Tibetan letter 'A' generates and the red color of the lotus. Asides from the letter 'A' at the center, each of the four petals also contains a Tibetan syllable. The petal facing the front of the body contains the 'RA' syllable. The petal facing the back has the 'SHA' syllable. The petal to the left side has the 'LA" syllable, and the petal to the right side has the 'SA" syllable. At this point, you should be feeling somewhat sleepy. Retain your calm concentration on the 'A' at the center of the lotus.

The purpose of this specific practice is to transfer our sense of energy and mind into the central passage. According to the teachings' instructions, focusing on the Tibetan letter 'A' means the practitioner's cultivation of peace. The resultant feeling of peaceful calmness should then be retained within oneself. The dreams that arise in this state are those of gentle occurrences. When you fall asleep in this state, you will dream of beautiful places, people, or even spiritual beings of peaceful essence. Such is the main aim of undergoing this practice.

DEVELOPING TRANSPARENCY

This is the second phase of the main practice, and it is done after about two hours of doing the first practice. Typically, this practice is done at midnight in Tibetan tradition, but due to our busyness with the samsaric affairs, it is better to arrange it according to our schedule.

Begin by maintaining the lion position as done in the first practice. For this practice, there are instructions to observe a particular pattern of breathing. The pattern is slightly tricky to envision, so it would be best to learn it physically from a teacher.

Inhale and gently hold the breath. Then, firmly contract your lower abdomen muscles to make it feel like forcing the withheld breath upwards. Think of the air as trapped in your lower abdomen, with no way to escape, and squashed with the constriction of your abdominal muscles.

Maintain this position for some time, then exhale calmly and slowly. While doing this, fully relax the constricted muscles. Do this seven times.

Here, our region of concentration is the chakra between the central forehead and the glabella. Imagine a sphere of white light in this region. The sphere of white light represents the compactness or rigidity of the energetic composition of the body.

As usual, simply imagining this ball of light is of little importance compared to feeling its presence and fusing with it in our visual sense. The transparency we feel at this moment is necessary for being able to envision the whole process efficiently.

As you merge with this ball of light, you experience a clear state of pure awareness. The connection of your essence with the luminosity of the sphere helps you to intensify your lucidity further. If you fall asleep at this point, you begin to experience the uninterrupted presence and full awareness in sleep and dreams.

BECOMING STRONGER

This is the third phase of the dream practice. The best time to perform it is approximately two hours after the previous exercise. That makes it about four hours after the initial sleep. Usually, this third practice should be done at about two hours till dawn. Again, we all have different timetables, so it is best to arrange them according to our schedule. The position to assume during this practice is somewhat different from the positions of the previous two courses.

Begin this practice by laying down with your head and neck on a pillow. Cross your legs. In this state, you should not cross your legs firmly like in meditation. Also, it is not essential if you place the right leg upon the left, or vice versa. This position should look like you are in a resting position, with your body leaned back against the pillow, although not wholly leveled with the bed. The protector should not be so high that it discomforts your neck. As this practice aims to cultivate a strengthened and continuous awareness, it is essential to make sure that the body is relaxed.

Afterward, inhale twenty-one times deeply. These inhalations should be as calm and gentle as possible, and you should pay utmost attention to your breathing process. Keep yourself aware of the breathing pattern.

Then make the chakra of the heart your point of focus. In the heart chakra, envision a black Tibetan syllable HUNG radiating light and facing the body's front. Then, with deep and uninterrupted presence, allow the HUNG syllable to fuse with the essence of your being. Feel the HUNG and the light merging with every inch of your body. Let the feeling become part of yourself, then begin to relax your mind calmly in this HUNG state. Once you have achieved this, you can now go to sleep.

The essence of this practice is to generate a sense of power. It is unnecessary to try to feel the surge of energy flowing through your body. This is not about becoming a superhero but rather about awakening the sense of power already inside you. This sense of power also has to do with the feelings of safety and protection. If a dream arises in this phase of practice, it would be a dream where you feel a sense of guaranteed security. It may be a dream where you are guarded by powerful dakinis or one in which you go to a secure settlement to perform practices or receive instructions. Either way, the primary point is the sense of power, safety, and protection when the practitioner dreams. Again, the specific occurrences of the dream may be irrelevant. The practitioner may experience phenomena where they are being celebrated, promoted, or appreciated, but in every plan, the goal is to develop power and security.

OVERCOMING FEAR

This is relatively the least difficult phase of the sleep practice. One does not have to assume any positions or training again till daylight. The body should just be relaxed. Also, breathing should be regular, as there is no particular breathing pattern to be undergone or maintained. This practice is about two hours after the third practice, that is, just before the morning twilight.

For this practice, the area of concentration is the chakra at the back of the nethers. This chakra is also known as the secret chakra. Then visualize a glowing ball of a black light (a black tiglé) just inside the chakra. According to the teachings, if a dream arises in this phase, the dream will be of furious beings, disastrous events, or elements that annihilate everything they come across. Try to learn if this is the same for you. In any case, the central point of this practice is to overcome the terror of the dreams.

After stabilizing and focusing on your imagination of the glowing, black tiglé, make the tiglé a part of you by merging with it. Enter it and let it flow through you in surges of distinct awareness. Then gently rest your mind and maintain scant attention on the beam of the black light present in your body, in your mind, everywhere. Then once more, in this state of uninterrupted awareness, let the power of sleep overcome you.

These four practices denote the four primary attributes of dream yoga; The sense of calmness, the purpose of awareness, the importance of security, and the sense of fearlessness. The experiences generated in the dreams we have during these practices are not what we should be concerned about. Instead, we should aim to pay attention to the emotional state of the dream. With this, we can determine the chakra from with the dream is generated, the realm with which the dream is associated, and the body's energetic components influencing the dream. All these cannot be determined if we get carried away by the contents of the dream.

After this fourth practice, you do not need to wake again until the start of the day. When you finally wake for the day, do not abandon the presence you have tried very hard to cultivate during the night. Maintain this sense of awareness throughout all your encounters and as you begin the practices for the day.

How Different Body Postures Affect Practice

During practice, we assume several positions to direct and channel our pranic components towards the specific practice. In Tibet, it is believed that the pranic components that channel negative emotions are connected with the fundamental energy passage on the left side of the women's body and the right side in men. b

For this reason, when a man sleeps on the left side, pranic passages on the right side are narrowed under his weight, while the channel on the left side becomes slightly widened. It also becomes relatively easier to inhale more air through the left naris.

As for women, the reverse is the case. They constrict the channel of negative prana when they sleep on their left side. Doing this helps to develop faster on the path to clarity and awareness.

The sense of maintaining meditation positions helps in the attainment of immense concentration during practice. One can utilize this technique all the time. When you suddenly find it difficult to focus in the middle of a practice, simply try adjusting your position or changing the posture completely. It helps to balance and stabilize the mind in the process of maintaining mental focus. Bearing in mind that the body posture, breathing pattern, pranic channeling, and the state of mind are all interconnected is helpful in the generation of positivity in the mind's deepest reaches.

The Mind's Concentration and Imagery

If you think of the four sleep practices as mere figments of imagination that do not exist, you are greatly mistaken. It is essential to know that when we visualize these things, be it an upright lotus, Tibetan syllables, or even a tiglé emitting lights of several colors, they are there, powered by our very sense of imagination. Envisioning these things is like imprinting their presence into our consciousness and innate perception, making us feel their presence as though they are staged physically before our eyes. That way, we allow our imaginations to affect our sense of awareness and how we perceive experiences. Apart from imageries of the mind and consciousness, color and light also play notable roles in affecting our consciousness. Even in the samsara, we tend to prefer specific colors to others. Subsequently, we adapt it to our ways of life; for instance, we often prefer to choose our favorite colors when we buy clothes or accessories. Similarly, the visualization of different colors influences the strength and intensity of our concentration during practices.

When we commit ourselves to dream yoga, our commitment level will determine the rate at which our sense of awareness is developed. Building the sense of conscious presence is not the same for everybody. Hence, we experience different levels of awareness. For instance, a practitioner that goes into retreat for years and one who meditates for months will both experience increased awareness and a sense of conscious presence, but just in varying intensities. The feeling of increased awareness of experiences is immediately identified due to the powerful perception of every detail. This happens not only in samsaric experiences but also in sleep and dreams. During our first sequence of practices, it feels challenging to maintain concentration on the Tibetan "A" or syllables through sleep inception. We feel ourselves losing our grip on the practical point of concentration as we slip into the darkness of sleep. But as time goes on, if we are consistent through the meditation processes, then it becomes more accessible, and dreams become more vivid, with every detail imprinted upon the practitioner's mind. Then we go to sleep while at the same time maintaining our awareness throughout the night's occurrences.

The process of changing and developing in this process is not easily noticeable. In many cases, amateur practitioners have stopped doing dream and sleep practices because they were unable to notice the results. These differences are too subtle to notice within the first few days of practice. But we begin to experience a feeling of heightened awareness and presence as we proceed with the cultivation of a more significant presence.

Just like sleep gets affected whenever certain occurrences are experienced in the samsara, we can also increase our awareness level by maintaining focus on feelings. For instance, if we need to settle a critical matter in the morning, say a matter of life and death, we would not be able to get our mind off the matter, even during sleep. The mind would be continuously preoccupied with the intensity of the matter, and once we wake, we would immediately become aware of the matter. The same happens when we experience something desirable during the day. The happiness and cheerfulness will follow us into our sleep. The mind will maintain that state, and when we wake, it would be to the awareness of the joy and cheerfulness of the previous day.

We can make practice easier by holding and maintaining concentration on the object of focus's visualized image as a feeling of positivity. That way, we become aware of it in a positive sense and being aware of it alone cheers us to proceed with practice. We would not forcefully hold on to the envisaged phenomena, say, the Tibetan letter "A." Rather, we keep it in a light and calm awareness. When we sleep, we do so, seeing everything as the Tibetan "A," we become dissolved in the awareness of the letter "A," and when we wake, we wake to full and unhindered awareness.

However, when we apply too much force into the process of concentrating, that is, when we forcefully hold on tightly to the imaginary point of focus, we may become too held to it that we find it difficult to sleep. This is not supposed to happen. We should consider the object of focus as a friend or companion present with us at that particular moment, merge with it and feel its presence in our awareness.

In envisioning the tiglé, making it appear actively in mind is just the preliminary step. Letting it penetrate your innate essence is the ultimate and the most seemingly tricky phase of the practice.

To make the practice easier to undergo, some master practitioners have given certain instances to beginners in dream yoga. Simply visualize a richly deep scarlet lotus in your throat chakra. Take note of the deep, glowing red light of its petals, feel the presence of the light in your throat chakra. Allow the light to stream through your mind. Let it purge your mind of samsaric disturbances. In your visualization, allow the scarlet light of wisdom to break the boundaries of your mind and let it radiate past your throat. Imagine the light spreading through your body, relaxing and healing your mind. Let the scarlet light fill you up so that each of your experiences disappears into the scarlet light. No thoughts, experience, or desires should be able to penetrate the healing power of the scarlet light. Abide in peacefulness and absolute calm as you allow the scarlet light to overwhelm you. Allow all of your feelings of negativities to melt into this light. Do not just confine this to your imagination; feel it in your innermost self. Experience it. The sounds you hear, the flow of breeze you feel, everything is now made of scarlet light. Nothing should be able to distract you now because there is no "you" to be distracted. There is no environment, no color, no form, no thoughts; everything is now dissolved in the light, and you exist with the scarlet light as a single unit! Like this, we say we have merged our essence with that of the lotus. If we fall asleep in this state, and a dream arises, it would be characterized by the essential attribute of the scarlet lotus. Similarly, we merge with the Tibetan letter "A" or Tibetan syllables when undergoing the sleep and dream practice of developing clarity and awareness.

Order of Practice

Undergoing each of these practices is a little like running a relay race. In a relay race, there are several athletes positioned at different points on the track. One athlete has to run as fast as they can to give the baton to the next athlete on the track, which means that the first athlete's success will undoubtedly contribute to the success of the second athlete and subsequently to the whole team. This is how it goes in these practices as well. One must do them in a sequential order to get the best of the desired results. However, even though undergoing these practices is of utmost importance, it is vital to pay attention to our state of health.

Occasionally missing some of these practices is practically inevitable, but it is critical to note that we cannot jump from one stage to another. If we miss the time for the second practice after doing the first practice but wake up in time for the third or fourth practice instead, we should still do the second practice. The process is a developmental one, so we should never try to skip a step. Even if you can only practice once, or twice, or even three times in an entire night, that is okay. The point is to maintain the order as well as the consistency in practice. Besides, do not cast yourself into distress just because you missed a practical step. It is not suitable for practice. Once you miss one of the four practices, calmly do it whenever you wake at night. It is pointless to fill the mind with negative emotions while at the same time attempting to clear them.

In the first phase of the practice, we are solely concerned with the cultivation of peaceful transparency and calmness. The associated chakra is the chakra of the throat. It is relatively the easiest part of the whole exercise. It is usually ubiquitous in every field of experience to start performing tasks from the most accessible parts. It is imperative to finish the first practice before trying to go on to further practices.

The second practice is usually done two hours after the first practice. You should have achieved the peacefulness and calmness required from the first phase of the practice before the second phase. The mind's state will have been prepared for the second stage of practice. The chakra used here is the chakra of the brow region, associated with the awakening and development of transparency. Undergoing this phase of sleep and dream practice will help develop the mind's transparency that the first practice has already stabilized. After this practice, there should be no shaking of concentration.

Then we wake again two hours before dawn for the third practice. For this practice, it is necessary to have enriched the mind with the first and second practices' attainments. Then, we proceed to accomplish power in the third phase of the practice. Here, we use the chakra of the heart, also known as the body's central chakra. The power we refer to is not some sort of violent or destructive power but the power to direct and control the mind and thoughts. The power makes it possible for us to deviate from the general trend of action and reaction, thereby maintaining our presence in the state of pure awareness. This kind of residual power can be related to a specific leader who resides in his abode of absolute power. You exist in absolute awareness, in the root of absolute power.

Then the fourth practice begins roughly two hours after the third. This practice is dependent on the success of the three previous practices, on the qualities of attaining equilibrium and calmness, transparency, and power. The fundamental characteristic of this fourth practice is the appearance of dreams based on the existence of furious beings and scary circumstances. The factors that cause the manifestations of these dream qualities are already inside of us. It only requires specific practice and conditions to evoke them in dreams. We let ourselves fall to sleep during the fourth practice with the highest possibility of having wrathful dreams by maintaining concentration on the secret chakra. This is because it is the chakra most associated with fear and fury. For the practitioner, the utility of this practice is not definite. We only have to consider it as a part of the teachings we have to practice to attain awareness. However, undergoing this practice helps develop the will-power, transparency, and stability of mind that we have generated in the previous practices. After consistent practices, the fearful dreams experienced in this fourth practice are no longer considered intimidating. Instead, they are utilized as a means of attaining spiritual growth.

Just observing the nature of sleep and dream yoga makes it look seemingly complex. But, as we undergo, to a high degree of proficiency, sleep and dream yoga principles, the practices become easier to do. The only requirement is to begin and proceed consistently. If you find it challenging to master all four practices at once, it is helpful to go with the first practice till you are stable enough to go further. You can simply just do the first practice at all waking hours of the night. Repeat this every night till you have attained enough stability. This way, the order of the practice will not be jeopardized. It will just be made simpler and more elongated. After getting through the first practice, you can then proceed to the second practice and repeat the same process. In short, it is very vital to practice in order, as each of the practices is based on the previous. For instance, the first practice is like a foundation for the second: the second, a foundation for the third. And the third, a foundation for the fourth.

For starters, especially nowadays teens, the whole process of sleep and dream yoga may seem uninteresting and boring. However, the importance and goodness of these practices cannot be overstated. And it is not until we fully experience it can we know how truly beneficial the practices are. As we go further in experiencing these practices of pure spiritualism, we become more appreciative of the teachings' wisdom. After we finally attain a stable awareness and a powerful sense of presence, we can then discontinue the primary practices since our aim is now achieved. Afterward, it is sufficient to just abide in the state of calm and pure awareness that we have cultivated with the four practices' experiences. If any dreams arise in this state of awareness, we will remain in presence since we have trained and heightened our minds' capacity during the basic practices.

The beginning of meditational practices is always the most difficult. Once we have attained lucidity, remaining in awareness while going on with everyday life activities will be as easy as driving a knife through hot butter.

Developing Your Capability of Lucid Dreaming

Attaining enlightenment is not a day's job. Notable masters in dream and sleep yoga have undergone retreats that last for days, months, and even years. Does this impress you? It should. Such masters have made the required effort to attain the state of truth, wisdom, and enlightenment. But today, with our habitual affinities with the samsaric affairs, we feel it is unfeasible to achieve such feat. This is not wrong in its entirety, but there is always an alternative to such problems. According to modern statistical science, an average person spends roughly 25 years of their life sleeping. This equates to about one-third of our lives. We can use the time that we spend sleeping to practice the teachings and ultimately attain enlightenment. By doing this, the impact of emotional inclinations that we experience during the emergence of dreams can be eradicated. For instance, while experiencing the dreams characterized by the appearance of wrathful beings and terrifying situations, we may feel scared or terrified. But as time goes on, with consistent practice, we can make ourselves impervious to such emotions that arise from dream experiences. When we have developed the ability to lucid dream, we can perform almost any practice in dreams, hence paving our path on the way to enlightenment.

Practicing the instructions of dream yoga improves the ability of everyone to lucid dream. To lucid dream means to dream in the state of pure awareness. In other words, when a dreamer is aware during a dream that he/she is dreaming, that is a state of clarity. However, it is possible to lucid dream without having the intention to do so: this has probably happened to most people. It may happen when we are having a terrible nightmare, and we struggle to avoid the resulting distress and tension by actively generating the intention to wake. Such occurrences may seldom occur in most cases, while in others, some people undergo lucid dreaming regularly without even knowing it or intending to do so. This proves that lucid dreaming is not some foreign habit we have to cultivate and blend into our lives. The practices are about developing the slight sense of transparency hidden inside us by practicing the instructions in the teachings. In the practices, our primary aspiration is not about attaining lucidity. Lucidity is just a significant development that we attain on the road to attaining enlightenment.

Lucidity is essential to practice because, in dreams, there is the absence of samsaric boundaries and limitations that confine us to certain restrictions in the waking experience. So, it is easier to perform practices and do anything we want to do in dreams. Therefore, to become a master in sleep and dream yoga, we need to develop lucidity. However, the development of transparency occurs in several degrees, depending on the factors surrounding our practice. At the beginning of dream practices, you may experience dreams with little sense of lucidity. For instance, you may be consciously aware that you are in a dream without any transparency or stability in the dream. This kind of transparency only favors the practitioner's awareness. All the other qualities required for practical lucid dreaming are unstable, not fully developed yet.

On the other hand, when masters of lucidity dream, they experience everything just as they appear in waking life. With increased transparency and more assertive presence, they can derive as much knowledge from the dream as they desire. With this lucidity intensity, you can perform virtually any form of practice in dreams that will reflect your waking life experience. This does not mean that if you obtain any corporeal blessing in dreams, such material will be yours when you wake. For instance, if you give birth to a baby in a dream and expect to find a baby next to you when you wake, you are wrong. Due to this bit of reality, we may think that since it is impossible to bring things and people from dreams into the *real*, waking life, it is similarly impossible to obtain any fundamental changes in dreams, no matter the level of clarity. This belief is wrong. When the good qualities of meditative experiences are developed, the practitioner can practice the teachings in dreams and extend the results into waking life. The resulting qualities of some practices are even more extensive when done in dreams than in waking life.

The most significant advantage of lucidity is that we can surmount the fixedness of the waking life in dreams. When we utilize the dynamism of dreams to get over the waking state's karmic boundaries, we start developing the suppleness of the mind, which is a vital part of experiencing spiritual progress. As an ordinary mind, without the taste of the meditative experience, the mind is stiff and stuffed with the very beliefs rooted in dualism itself.

This book is the best guide in learning to diminish our dualistic acts of acknowledgment and repulsion. This continuum of chronic negative emotions helps us get trapped within the limits of our ignorance. We refuse to get enlightened due to the constrictions in our minds. We become restrained to specific experiences without any suppleness of the mind whatsoever. All these arise from the base of our ignorant minds. When we develop the mind's suppleness, our ability to control our experiences without utilizing habitual means of reacting becomes fully developed. Also, we begin to reduce the rate at which we welcome karmic traces by indulging in dualistic perception. With time and consistent practice, the habit of acknowledgment and repulsion can become fully diminished.

Like lucidity, there are several levels to the manifestation of karmic dualism in different people's behaviors. Some people get highly attached to every experience they encounter, but other people only get lightly attached. This will determine the degree to which we are being tossed back and forth by the manifestations of karmic traces. This is why it is critical to developing the mind's suppleness by undergoing fundamental and significant sleep and dream yoga practices. Doing these practices will help us on the path towards enlightenment and help us develop a sense of positivity. Only then can we be able to react to experiences in a non-dualistic manner. That is, without engaging the emotional negativities of acknowledgment and repulsion. We then entertain thoughts without getting attached to them in any way. This process can be compared to a pool. Everyone goes into the pool to either refresh their body and mind or for recreational purposes. Throughout every process, the pool welcomes everyone without demonstrating any form of attachment or discrimination. In this way, the pool is kept at peace. Even when there is turbulence, it would all eventually end up in absolute calm. Let your mind be like the pool. Think of distractions and thoughts as the people that go into the pool whenever they wish. Allow thoughts and conditioned experiences to flow in, and let them dissolve in your state of pure non-dualism (rigpa).

Once we have attained lucidity, we can begin to dream without being restrained by waking life's constrictions. This means that to attain good suppleness and flexibility of the mind, we have to experience situations that are not governed by our samsaric life's boundaries. We can begin by transforming everything we encounter, by performing all sorts of tasks that would otherwise have been impossible in the waking state. Like this, we start to expose ourselves to all the possibilities of the universe and develop the suppleness of the mind. Then all these start to reflect in the waking life. We become less attached to all sorts of emotional hindrances, and we dissolve them in our state of awareness.

When we learn to transform and alter several dream experiences as per our wish, we can apply the same technique to the waking state's emotional negativities. We can alter any form of emotion and prevent ourselves from being affected by the emergence of karmic experiences. Consistently undergoing these practices helps us escape the underlying negativities embedded in our emotions and beliefs, to experience the world in a crystal-clear manner, in apparent details, just like in dreams. Thus, our ability to make positive choices with the suppleness of the mind is greatly heightened.

Attaining Suppleness

Before one can decide to extend the mind further past the restrictions of samsaric bondage, we must first have undergone the process of attaining pure awareness in sleep −that is, absolute clarity. This is because lucidity is required to tread the path of achieving the mind's suppleness.

So, after developing oneself in the process of lucid dreaming, we can then proceed to the first stage of expanding our mind's suppleness − knowing of our ability to increase the suppleness of the mind. This is the way of recognizing it as one of the things we are capable of. Automatically, we find that, with little effort, our mind readily stretches to the points that we never envisioned before. We find ourselves lucid-dreaming and making things happen – things that we never thought we could do. That is the way of the mind: show it how to achieve a particular feat, and you will discover that just little effort is required.

In the typical samsaric dimension of existence, it is almost impossible for a person to go a day without thinking about many things. Even as a child, you have probably had experiences of getting preoccupied or worried about one or two things simultaneously. This string of thoughts divides the mind's focus and concentration. It is like having to defeat two mean opponents at the same time. One has a very high chance of losing unless the mind in question is a solid one. However, instead of having to split mental awareness, we can undergo the practice of complete self-division in dreams. While lucid-dreaming, it is feasible to divide your body into several vessels of existence. This dream practice is just a form of upgrade to the transformation practice described above. You create multiple versions of objects that you encounter in dreams. But for you to be able to do this, you must have been through the first essential step –recognizing your possibility of being able to achieve the feat in the first place. If you do not think of yourself as capable of doing the transformation practice, you have confined yourself to certain limitations, and to you, it is impossible to transform. These limitations are those that only exist in the samsara. Thus, you become restrained to specific experiences in dreams and the waking state. This is not supposed to be. Instead, it should be the other way round. We should retain the knowledge that dreams are dynamic and recognize that we can do and undo anything in dreams –anything we think of doing. That is the essence of dream practice.

Dreams have been used to attain and develop skills and obtain knowledge since the earliest ages. Recently, western researchers have discovered that it is indeed possible to develop skills and abilities when we practice them in dreams. This proves the level of authenticity of the instructions contained in the teachings. Ancient masters utilized dreams to decrease their negativity levels and increased the positive. By doing this, they were able to get rid of the residual string of reactions to experiences. We can also apply this process to overcome both spiritual obstacles and problems that are characteristic of samsaric roots.

The teachings highlight eleven distinct varieties of experience in which we can develop the mind and attain stability. With each of these experiences, the goal is to identify the restriction, face it, and transform it. This is how we overcome all the restrictions. However, it is pointless to rush. We should spend enough time on each experience to reflect on it and create the possibility of being able to transform and expand the experience.

The varieties of experiences are size, speed, quantity, quality, accomplishment, transformation, emanation, journey, sight, encounter, and experiences.

Size: In this aspect of the experience, there can either be two possibilities: small or big. Transform yourself as well as the objects around you. Make a tiny object as large as a giant, and transform a large field of haughty grasses into a small garden of adorable flowers. Transform yourself as well. Observe how it feels when you are as tall as a mountain and what happens when you are as tiny as a small ant.

Speed: In dreams, it is possible to alter the speed at which time passes. You can do a vast number of things in the space of just one minute. Make every experience of your dream worth living by slowing it down and assimilating all details. There is nothing you cannot do. The only limit is that which is in your head.

Quantity: In this frame of experience, if you encounter a single piece of goodness in dream practice, multiply it and make it a million. If you encounter a million undesirable situations, merge everything and make them one. This is the key to destroying the karmic seeds that are yet to manifest. Be in control of your dream rather than let yourself be controlled by the dream.

Quality: As stated earlier, your dream practice must be based on knowing that all the characteristics of a dream are subject to change. With this, it would be impossible for you to get stuck with negative emotions. In dreams, whenever you feel hatred, transform it into compassion and love. Believe that you can do this without any difficulty. If you find it hard to convince yourself, say it out loud to make it easier. Once you have developed the ability to transform emotions in dreams, you can do it while in the waking state. Accomplishing this is a significant achievement in sleep and dream yoga, for you are no longer imprisoned with the leash of negative karmic emotions.

Accomplishment: There is quite an endless number of impossible tasks to overcome in the waking state, but again, all these are very feasible in dreams. Accomplish whatever you want to accomplish in your dreams. Undergo very complex practices, travel around the world, develop your singing skills, and do whatever you desire.

In the case that we find it challenging to accomplish a task, it is helpful to call upon our guardians for assistance. If you are eventually successful in the dream, you will feel joyful, and this happiness will reflect in your experiences when you wake.

Transformation: To accurately practice the instructions of the teachings, transformation is a vital field of experience. Its importance as the implicit root of all tantric practices cannot be over-emphasized. In dream practices, transform yourself into various things. Try to turn into a god, an animal, or a demi-god. If you feel angry, transform your angry self into a being filled with love and compassion. If you feel scared, transform your frightened self into a courageous and fearless person. Transform yourself into various deities, elements, and dakinis. Transform your dualistic self into a clear-minded, non-dualistic deity. As you do these, you empower your mind with pure and absolute suppleness.

Emanation: Like transformation, this stage also involves transmogrifying yourself into another shape. However, in this case, after transforming yourself into a deity (a buddha, for example), you project yourself into many more bodies. Project your consciousness into two bodies, then an indefinite number of bodies, and then more. Doing this allows you to overcome the consideration of yourself as just one unit of consciousness.

Journey: Here, you will be able to go anywhere that you ever wished to visit. Do you like the view of the statue of liberty in movies? Travel to New York. Go wherever you have the intention to visit. This does not mean that you disappear, then appear at the place you wish to visit. You have to navigate yourself there actively. With this knowledge, you can decide to travel anywhere you wish. Anywhere. Be it other realms of existence or the top of a mountain.

Sight: In your dreams, you can see the things that you have always wished to see. Even the beings that are only visible in the deepest parts of dream practice can be seen. You can see dakinis and deities. You can see blood flowing through the channels in your body and nerves passing electric currents. Just form the idea in your mind, and it will become real in your dreams.

Encounter: Earlier in this book, we have learned about a man who had various encounters with dakinis and masters from whom he obtained vast knowledge and experience. Do you feel the need to meet masters in ancient times? You can now create an encounter with them, and when this happens, immediately ask for permission to meet them at other times. If they agree, then you can create encounters with them again and receive teachings from them.

Experience: Here, you can use the fluidity of dreams to experience any situation you have not encountered yet. If you are having doubts about your non-dualistic experiences' stability, then practice it in dreams to make sure. You can experience various categories of arcane situations. You can go to the deepest parts of the ocean and abide there. You can bleat like a goat, fly like a bird, strike the earth like thunder, walk on water. You are capable of doing and experiencing vast measures of conditions. As long as you recognize this fact, you can do anything.

Consider the categories of experience stated above as just outlines of what we must overcome. Drive your exploratory senses further past the limits of the experience categories. The existence of these limits in our minds keeps us from exploring the space of experience beyond our understanding level. To make peace with the fact that there is no limit of expectations in dreams means finally discovering the essence of our natural mind. If you encounter a problem in your dreams, transform yourself into the solution and annul the problem. If you get troubled by destructive forms of natural elements like fire, water, or wind, transform yourself into something more remarkable and more tremendous. For example, if you get threatened by a destructive fire, transform yourself into flames as hot as the blasts of a volcano. If you encounter a menacing fiend, transform yourself into a gigantic form of demon. There are a vast number of things with which you can experiment. You can turn into a body of water, or an iroko tree, a lion, a soaring hummingbird. You can turn yourself into an entire planet, and you can travel through the universe in majestic beams of sunlight. You can even transform your gender. For instance, if you are a man, you can turn into a woman or a beautiful goddess. If you are a woman, you can become a man or a powerful deity. Transform into animals as legendary as dinosaurs. Transform into the buddha and project your consciousness into thousands of that version. In tantric transformations, we have to undergo a series of practices similar to this one. Those tantric practices involve the envisioning of yourself as something else. That is, you transform only in the imaginative sense. In these dream practices, you transform into varieties of things and observe experiences from that view.

You can visit wherever you desire to visit. Travel through the earth and into the various realms. Float through hell and the god realm. The purpose of all this is to release the constrictions of your mind. You will not be participating in the experiences of the realms you travel through; it will only help in the disengagement of limitations from your mind.

In the zhine practices of meditation with the Tibetan letter "A," the letter's form and structure are unnecessary. Still, the awareness of it being there is the type of focus required for the meditation. Similarly, in dream practices, the specific details are not the main point. The suppleness that the mind acquires during these practices is the primary goal of practice. There should not be any boundaries to your mind's capabilities. When you discover limits in any quality of experience, form new ideas in your mind and overcome the limits. Bring this flexibility into your waking life. Whenever you encounter samsaric experiences that are hazardous to your mental stability and active awareness, you should transform it in its entirety into pure transparency.

Even when we have achieved the mind's suppleness, it is still vital that we continue to practice. This is the fundamental basis of every yogic activity –continuity and consistency. There are wide varieties of experiences to undergo in dreams. We can go to any length, pull any plug, meet any being, transform anything, do any practice, all without any restrictions. However, whatever we do in dreams, we must always choose the positive side. These practices are based on banishing opposing forces and choosing the positive, so it is pointless to attain clarity and still use dreams to entertain negativities. To deviate from the path of negative emotions towards positivity is to make ourselves ready for enlightenment. As said earlier, everything we do in dreams becomes imprinted upon our way of life, even in the waking state. We experience total freedom to do anything in dreams, but we are not free from karmic manifestations of emotions and experiences until we get rid of our dualistic nature. To do this, we must maintain a clear intention and passionate consistency to acquire the extreme suppleness required to expel the hostile karmic forces from the mind.

The power of your mind is incredible. With sufficient time and consistent practice, it can overcome almost any obstacle. Knowing this, you can effectively diminish your mind's karmic boundaries by practicing in dreams and bringing the positive effects into samsaric experiences. All you need to do is realize that you can do it. Then it has become doable in all possibilities. Your mind is more flexible than you think it is. When people tell themselves that they cannot do something, even if they try, most times, they fail. In contrast, if you believe that you can do a particular thing, you have already finished the first part of the exercise.

At all times, do regard dreams with honor and make all encounters in dreams a means of integrating the teachings into our lives. When you utilize dreams to attain freedom from karmic boundaries, to develop the suppleness of mind, to triumph over hindrances that you encounter, and lastly to identify and acknowledge your primordial nature and the actual, transparent nature of all experiences, we say that you are taking full advantage of the dream's potential.

Hindrances Associated With Dream Practice

According to the Tantric teachings, four significant hindrances may be impedimental to one's progress in the practice of dream yoga: diversion of attention in spurious phantasm, leniency, restiveness, and forgetfulness. This chapter emphasizes how these hindrances can be avoided and fixed with both extrinsic corrections and internal remedies.

DELUSIVE DISTRACTION

This hindrance arises when an internal or external distraction diverts our focus away from the practice and towards the specific element of distraction itself. The distractions may be in the form of noise, or images, or even experiences. During practice, when we hear a sound, for example, the mind first scans the sound that made the noise, then some connection is established between the mind and the sound. This connection may be based on familiarity, curiosity, or even the memories of the practitioner's mind. Then we begin to lose concentration as the mind edges away from the essence of the practice and towards the elusive fantasy of distraction.

The internal remedy to this is to bring back awareness into the channel at the center. Just try and focus on the central passage's pranic composition, and you will feel your mind stop fantasizing about the delusional distractions. While doing this, go easy on yourself. You need not get pointlessly worked up, thereby making the practice hard for yourself. Maintain peace and calmness while simultaneously stabilizing your awareness as you focus on the central pranic channel.

You can also try to realize, in the meditative state, the importance of abiding in the pure, clear light state of monism (rigpa). This will help retain presence and focus during practice.

The external state's remedy is to do an immensely spiritual practice like 'guru yoga' or perform an oblation.

LENIENCY

This is the second form of hindrance that can obscure or dim our concentration while undergoing specific practices. This obstacle surfaces during practice as a form of lazy negligence. In this case, the intensity of power and transparency required to maintain focus on the practice is absent. The practitioner feels lazily lax and weak on the inside, unable to penetrate the dimness of his/her mind. Unlike the first hindrance, this hindrance prevents the mind from being capable of pursuing any distraction. The mind is just there, with a vague focus and a comfortable sense of presence.

The internal remedy to this problem is envisioning a shadowy form of blue vapor easily moving up from the three primary channels' merging point through the central channel. As you visualize this, do not get needlessly lost in the useless details of the vapor's motion. Visualize it actively moving up gracefully through the central passage.

The external antidote is to request that a master or teacher help you perform an exorcism. This is because the teachings propose that obstruction spirits may cause this kind of negligent behavior.

RESTIVENESS

Being restive may be caused by feelings of too much excitement or trepidation or pranic imbalance in the body.

The internal remedial practice is to visualize protective dakinis in the form of luminous Tibetan syllables imprinted upon the petals of a beautiful red lotus resting upon your throat chakra. The 'RA' syllable is yellow and faces the front of the body. The 'LA' syllable is green, and to the left side, the 'SHA' syllable is red and faces the back of the body. The SA syllable is blue and to the right side. We should envision these syllables whenever we feel restive and unable to focus while sleeping. Feel the power of protective dakinis covering you from all angles.

The external remedy is to do the Bon practice of Chod and try to offer sacrifices to beings and spirits. Also, search your memories to determine if you have a pending or abandoned form of duty or responsibility you may have promised someone.

In the case that you may need to confess a sin, do the practice of guru yoga and admit your guilt to The Master in wholeheartedness. If you did something wrong, make up your mind not to repeat such a thing. If you have a problem with a friend or companion, you can discuss the matter with them. This will help to lighten your mind and free you of the burden that would have hindered you from concentrating during practice.

FORGETFULNESS

This is the fourth form of hindrance that impedes progress during the sleep and dream yogic practices. The practitioner may forget the occurrences of their dreams or even forget to practice at all. Even if one encounters advantageous experiences in dreams –for instance, obtaining teachings from a master, it may still be forgotten.

We can cure this situation by going into a long and quiet retreat. One can also observe calming breathing practices before undergoing the primary practice to help battle the hindrance of forgetfulness.

Another form of remedial action is doing the first phase of sleep practice, as explained in earlier chapters. As you envision the Tibetan 'A,' watch out for the other obstacles stated above. Maintain concentration on the red letter 'A' and keep it in light awareness as you begin to fall asleep. Doing this will make it easier for you to remember whatever occurs during the night.

The problems encountered during practices are not limited to the ones stated above. Other hindrances that may be encountered include an imbalance of the prana, disturbance from local spiritual beings, and sickness.

Recognizing, Managing, And Utilizing Dreams

In some western communities, it is considered toxic to try and control the experiences in dreams. According to this belief, dreams are a projection of thoughts and emotions in the unconscious self, and we should not tamper with them. This opinion acknowledges the existence of the unconscious self, capable of organizing strings of distinct experiences whose meaning is either apparent or in need of illustrative representation.

Dreams exist in the space and context of the unconscious mind, and we recognize and find meaning to it with the help of the conscious mind. The meaning given to the phenomena in dreams will determine how the particular dream will be utilized. As explained earlier, there are various uses of dreams. These uses include but are not limited to: balancing the state of mind and the pranic components of the body, meeting masters and receiving teachings from them, developing the mind's suppleness, and diagnosing sicknesses. To successfully develop the ability to relate the projections of the unconscious mind with the conscious mind's attributes, one must have understood the dynamism of both states. To a large extent, everything is eventually given meaning by attaining enlightenment.

When practicing with dreams, we try to obtain the particular impression connected with the dream. This is not considered wrong by most practitioners. It has been a widespread belief that the knowledge derived from dreams is used in various aspects of life. Dreams, as we experience them, do not project meaning directly to the practitioner. The practitioner casts the idea that of meaning unto the dream and then makes out the meaning from the dream. The meaning of a dream is determined by certain factors which depend on the individual experiencing it. It is not until we feel the need to find meaning to a dream that the meaning reflects. So, if two practitioners have the same dream, each of them may infer distinctively different meanings from the dream. This proves that there is no third-party unit that influences or shapes the meaning of a dream.

To make use of the concept of sleep and dream as a means of attaining enlightenment, we need to fully and thoroughly grasp the concept of what a dream truly means. To do this, we need to have an excellent understanding of experiences and how to influence them. As we proceed into the deeper depths of dream practice, using the instruction in the teachings as a guide, we experience several amazing dreams, denotive of how far we have gone on the journey to attaining absolute epiphany. At this point, we may have realized that the meaning of a dream is not significant. However, before we get to this point of realization, it is helpful not to think of dreams as a projection of information and experience from another entity upon your unconscious self or from some subconscious region of your body of which you are not aware. It is due to our dualistic minds that we form meanings to every experience in the samsara. When we have attained the state of pure non-dualism (rigpa), we will understand this better concept better, although it is best to dispose of the idea of meaning before that time. This does not mean that we should become confused or unordered in the things we do. Like many others, the concepts of meaning and its contrasting form do not exist when one has attained monism. We only view things in their proper, transparent, and light-based state when we are at the essential base of clarity ourselves. This is what we aim to achieve with the practices of dream yoga.

Although we are not indifferent to the inferential meaning, we still need to understand that we are also dreaming of the meaning. Rather than consider dreams' meanings as a necessity, why not go into the aspects more significant than meaning? This is the root of experience that forms the fundamental essence of spiritual realization. At this point, you do not care about the underlying theme of the dream. You are not affected by the string of forces that arise from the interactive processes based on dualism that occur within your mind. You have achieved the more advanced form of dream yoga.

As implied earlier, the experiences encountered in dreams and their influences follow us into the waking state. Similarly, as we experience several forms of encounters in the waking state, the influences become apparent in dreams. Using this technique, most dream yoga practices are done in the waking state to manipulate the dream further. This way, we are not making changes to the dream in a straightforward sense. When we talk of manipulating dreams directly, we talk of lucid dreaming. We do all sorts of practices like transformation and the projection of thoughts, consciousness, and presence into other beings with clarity. According to the teachings, doing this helps develop the mind's suppleness and further stabilize one's perception of a wide variety of experiences. The mind's suppleness attained during dream practice is also extended to the waking life, but not for transformation and the other practices done while lucid-dreaming. All these cannot be done in the waking state due to the limitations of the samsaric dimension. The mind's suppleness is applied in the waking state to comprehend the integral state of experience and the subsequent sense of wisdom. Instead of allowing your feelings and emotions to dictate your sense of perception and, subsequently, your reaction to experiences, it is better to subject ourselves to something different. Control the way you feel about dreams and experiences, and you will find that your life is no more based on the manifestations of karmic traces. This will even reflect in your dreams.

Karmic traces give rise to the emergence of samsaric occurrences. The way we respond to these occurrences gives rise to further karmic traces, making the whole process a string of unending loops for a dualistic mind. Dreams are not exempted from this principle, either. Therefore, it is crucial to react to experiences not from our feelings and emotions but from the base of our active consciousness.

In the west, it is a widespread belief that we should not tamper with dreams. They believe that when a dream arises, it does so with the unconscious part of ourselves that is best left alone. This is a wrong impression indeed. From the point of achieving the simple meditational process to the point of doing the complex practices in pure transparency, we are not impeding the message being passed to us by the subtle parts of ourselves, as most westerners would claim. There is no message other than that which we project unto the dream by ourselves. By altering dreams' form and experiences, we are increasing the mind's flexibility while simultaneously burning the seeds of ignorance from our minds.

Simplification Of Sleep And Dream Yoga

In sleep and dream yogic practices, several factors determine one's progress. These factors are belief, aim or goal, patience, and devotion. These practices require time and consistent effort to reflect in our individual lives. It is impossible to achieve the result of a practice in one night. There is the time factor. We need to be patient and consistent with the practical exercises to achieve notable progress. During these practices, it is pointless to battle against time. Surely you would lose if you do. Although the human mind is potent indeed in might and capabilities, it is useless to force it to adapt to situations in a short period.

The whole of these yogic activities may seem too arduous a task for our assimilation when we learn about them. But, to make the practices easier to do, there are ways we can simplify and split them into different aspects of our lives. This way, we adapt more quickly.

Throughout the waking period of the day, the mind is actively crowded with business or activities. Sometimes, we even feel that the waking period hours are not enough for us when we spend all the time in delusion and disagreeable situations. In recent times, there are many distractive activities and situations that steal our concentration and make staying in awareness near to impossibility. Nowadays, each day's hustle and bustle are so overwhelming that we find it extremely difficult to practice for even some hours. From the necessity of caring for one's family to the stress of jobs and social interaction, we are driven to tiredness every day. This sort of lifestyle is not very good for practicing dream yoga. The essence of sleep and dream yogic practices is to cultivate more presence in ourselves, achieving and maintaining bodily and spiritual wholeness. This cannot be achieved by living a life that tears you away from yourself every day. A life in which you live in a blur of events that result in the preoccupation of the mind, sleeping trouble, and dreams controlled by karmic traces. To prevent this, we need to start doing some uncomplicated practices to get back within ourselves and cultivate more awareness.

There are easy exercises that help in the cultivation of more awareness. We can even turn every inhalation into practice. Every breath we take can be utilized to expel negativities and regain awareness when it is lost. To do this, breathe normally, but in continuous presence and awareness. As you breathe in, visualize good, positive energy coming in with the air you are taking. Then as you breathe out, envision all the negative energies, tension, and hindrances flow out of your body with the air you are exhaling. This practice is perfect for relaxing the body, especially in times of distress. It can be done anywhere and anytime. You can do it when your boss vexes you, or you can do it when you get worried about somebody you care for, or when you are sitting at the café doing nothing, or when you are out with your mates.

Another simple but very efficient practice is to preserve awareness of your body's wholeness consistently. The human mind is difficult to tame. It is not an easy task to focus on one thing at a time, especially when you have many things to take care of, like most people these days. However, we can use our body as a reminder to regain our awareness and abide calmly in it. As we continuously do this, we begin to detect whenever we lose focus and then regain it without getting reminded. Subsequently, our awareness is cultivated, and we start to live in pure and absolute presence.

It is necessary for the mind to remain active for the body to function effectively. Similarly, it is necessary for the body to be active so the mind can function effectively. This is a vital point that we need to understand before and while undergoing any practice. Therefore, we need to take these simple practices seriously to help generate more awareness and prepare our minds for more advanced practices. These practices have so many upsides. That is, you can practice them just about anywhere while doing almost anything and at any time. As you abide by consistency with these practices, you become more present in the occurrences of space and time: you do things with more awareness. When you admire something beautiful, everything you see at that specific moment is the beauty of that thing. When you read, you read with utmost awareness. This way, you remember things very quickly, and cultivating good habits become a part of you. But as stated before, no practice ever produces favorable results in a day. To achieve valid results, one has to be consistently patient and unrelenting. That is the only way you can become a successful spiritual practitioner.

While doing the simple practices, train your mind to experience events. Your clarity in dreams depends on your awareness during the day, so, for transparency and clarity during dreams, it is helpful to try as much as possible to maintain a complete presence during the day. When you look at something, look at it in awareness; when you walk, walk with awareness; when you smell something, do so with uninterrupted awareness. Do not keep doing something physically while your mind is traveling somewhere else. Make it a priority to be in awareness at all times.

Even as you develop your senses with these practices, you will still experience some mind distractions. You may be looking at a blue object for a moment. Next, your mind is digging up distractions connected to the blue color or even about the object in question. When this happens, try to disconnect your mind from the distraction and focus your awareness on the object. Distraction by lots of samsaric occurrences has become a standard form of experience to most people. Our goal as dream yogis is to get rid of those behaviors and cultivate new, advantageous habits in their place. Then we can experience the world in pure, vivid awareness. Whenever we base our awareness of something, we establish a connection between us and the object that no form of distraction would be able to break. We make use of such connections in meditation and while attaining lucidity.

Unification of All Practices

Your decision to choose to perform these practices should be based solely on attaining enlightenment in all aspects of the world. A practitioner of these dream practices is bound to be regarded that way by the individual elements and the world as a whole. One does not just undergo these practices for personal development or as a subject of fascination. To choose these sleep and dream practices is to choose the spiritual path that ultimately leads to enlightenment. So, the practitioner learns to unify the teachings with his/her life. All these processes have already been explained in the previous chapters. So, only the summary will be available here.

The summation of all dream practices is divided into two general phases. The first phase deals with the mind's dualism, while the second phase is absolute monism. The first phase is based on practices like the preparatory meditative practices, primary sleep and dream occurrences, transformation in dreams, cultivation of awareness, application of dream practices to the waking life and vice versa, attainment of transparency, etc. It forms the root of all the fundamental practices in sleep and dream yoga. In this phase of practice, we take into account all the experiences in dreams and those of the waking hour regarding our practices.

However, in the practices involving the state of pure monism (rigpa), the experiences in dreams and those in the waking hours do not matter. One abides in utmost clarity and observes the universe's elements in their pure, genuine, clear-light state.

The world we all live in −or rather, virtually all of us− is mixed with various dualism tools. The goals, views, beliefs, culture, religion, and the other establishments of the human race are all based on the concept of dualism. Therefore, to walk along the spiritual path and attain outstanding achievements, we have to appreciate dualism in its precise form to be successful in our spiritual practices. Since the samsara is filled with dualism, and we need to perform our practices in the samsara automatically, we need to get accustomed to the essence of dualism to accomplish our goal. As we undergo the dream and sleep practices, we learn how to abandon dualism and embrace our true selves. We learn to transform negative karmic emotions and feelings into something more positive. For instance, we learn to transform anger into compassion, hatred into love, weakness into great strength, and fear into toughness and courage. Our ability to work together with the forces of the world then becomes extensively developed. Our progress in practice is not impeded, and we also do various things to benefit others. All these are conditioned by our view of the world as fluid and flexible, just like it is in dreams. Only a believer of this sentiment can develop the ability to transform the world from the stressful, repelling state into a place beautiful and adorable nature. With this, we begin to dedicate all our features of spiritualism to the path.

However, we cannot indeed be free from the clutches of good and evil, positive and negative, right or wrong, the need for meaning, and dualism in its entirety until we fully dissolve our ordinary selves into the state of rigpa. The truth and wisdom associated with the non-dualistic state of mind are beyond the conditioning of all dualism elements. When you suppose that you have achieved the state of monism, but your dualistic mind still conditions you, you begin to live a life of unbalanced spirituality because you believe something different than what you actually practice. However, when you dissolve into a pure and absolute state of rigpa, no form of negative energy can condition your reality, and you can easily determine if you have achieved it.

In the unification of dream practices, we recognize four distinct and practical classes: sight, dream, bardo, and clear light. The sight is the summation of all the encounters we have had both in the samsara and in dreams, all the experiences we were part of, and all the internal pranic occurrences that condition our reality. We attain sight in dreams when we develop the ability to become present in dreams and maintain the state of awareness throughout the dream. True and pure unification of this state with the waking state brings about an effect in the practitioner's life. This includes how the practitioner reacts to the affairs of the world. Also, the level of the dualism of that practitioner is reduced. That is, the practitioner begins to observe the world in a less dualistic manner.

Similarly, they experience fewer obstacles that arise from emotional inclinations. All that once seemed to be enchanting and alluring then become empty and meaningless as we find ourselves abiding in awareness.

All the changes that occur during the waking state, resulting from more awareness, are then incorporated into dreams. Although we attain lucidity itself in dreams, all the other factors conditioning the dream arise from the waking state. Lucid dreaming is not compressed into a whole process: there are sequential stages of lucidity. At first, one becomes aware of being in a dream, but the practitioner does not fully control the dream's subtle experiences. From there, we develop our clarity in dreams until we reach the ultimate stage. In this stage, there is complete freedom to modify and transform the dream's occurrences while experiencing the dream itself with absolute clarity.

Then, as the thoughts and emotions generated during the day are used to influence dreams, the experiences of dreams are used to prepare for the intermediate state after death (bardo). Dying is a little like falling asleep, and the state after death is similar to entering a dream. Of course, it is essential to maintain non-dual awareness after death, too, and your chance of abiding in a state of non-dualism during bardo is determined by your level of achievements in dream yoga practices. When you practice in dreams, you prepare yourself for the death and the intermediate state that follows it. This involves the unification of all dream experiences into the bardo and knowing that the effects of all your activities in dreams will be the same as or similar to the effects of your actions in the intermediate state after death. Therefore, we must attain a kind of lucidity with which we can observe dreams in crystal clear form and uninterrupted awareness because it is upon this ability that our capability to stay aware after death is based.

The clear light is the next most ultimate stage of dream yoga after the successful preparation for bardo. We are to unify the bardo together with the clear light to reach the final means of attaining enlightenment. While still experiencing bardo, we cannot relate to the events that occur in a dualistic manner. Instead, we should abide by complete awareness and uninterrupted concentration. With this, we unite with the clear light. This is the combination of the void and absolute and conscious presence. If we are able to do this before death, then we have reached the final stage of dream practice in the living state. When we completely dissolve in the pure state of rigpa and unify with the clear light, we stop dreaming.

When we develop lucidity to a certain point, we recognize the dream-like state of the waking period. This form of lucidity eventually manifests in dreams, and we become aware while dreaming as well. When we develop and stabilize our lucidity in dreams up to a certain point, it manifests in the bardo. When we abide in full monism during bardo, we become enlightened. This is the summary of the general practice.

As you continue to apply dream practices consistently, you will realize the influence in your waking life. If you undergo the full practices from the start to the end and succeed, the outcome is liberation. That is, you get wholly and absolutely enlightened. If it so happens that you do not see any changes in your waking life experiences as a result of lucid dreaming, then there must be some kind of obstacle inhibiting your progress in the yogic practices. You have to inquire about the obstacle and determine the best way to get rid of it. You can also visit a master for guidance on how to go about it. If there is still no form of progress, then you should check within yourself and strengthen your intent. When you finally achieve progress, be grateful, receive and integrate them into your life with great joy. Then use these phenomena to back up your intent further, and you will continue to achieve progress in the yogic practices.

PART FOUR

THE CONCEPT OF SLEEP

Losing Oneself To Sleep

The whole sequence of falling asleep begins with a slight loss of awareness in everything. Then gradually, the conscious mind wears into the regular unawareness of the ordinary mind. The occurrence of thoughts and mental activities then ceases until there is no bit of our conscious self left. The state of unconsciousness then takes over, and we stay in this state till dreams start to occur. When dreams arise, we partly regain self-consciousness due to our mind's acknowledgment and repulsion with the contents of the dream. This sense of consciousness is then lost again following the dream and regaining back when another dream arises. Our loss and regaining of consciousness make up the entire process of a typical night's sleep.

Our loss of consciousness upon falling asleep gives us the impression of darkness. There is no registered experience during this period because the conscious mind which constitutes our identity at that particular moment has been deactivated. This happens at the exact moment we fall asleep. When it happens, we say that we "lose ourselves to sleep." When we dream, this conscious self becomes awakened again, hence recognizing that we are in a dream.

Most people would say that the darkness and unconsciousness that comes with sleep are sleep's most essential natures. This doesn't seem right indeed. When we have dissolved into absolute, non-dual awareness, there is nothing like sleep. There is only the integration of everything with the clear light, which is our minds' actual nature. It is through this state that we overcome all sorts of ignorance and our dualistic existence. We attain freedom from feelings, emotions, thoughts, negativities, karma, ignorance, and dreams. There is no form of samsaric or even mental distraction that can influence us in this state. It is the actual state of the mind where profound truth and wisdom are attained. The only thing that arises in this state is the absolute calm we abide by, peacefulness, and utmost transparency. It is not until we develop the ability to stay in this kind of awareness that we will truly understand sleep's luminosity. The darkness becomes overcome by our clear light awareness, and we get to maintain spiritual stability in our true nature.

Karmic traces are the elements that give rise to dreams. The in-depth explanations of how this happens have been given in previous chapters. The entire process of how the manifestation of karmic traces result in dreams, how our dualistic responses condition dreams to the dream's events, and how to self-liberate negative emotions to become free from being restrained by the influence of karmic traces have been described in details earlier. When we attain lucidity, not only are we aware of being in a dream, we also develop the ability to take part in the dream's events actively and ultimately become the primary influencer of the dream, rather than karmic traces.

However, our perception of sleep is different from that of a dream, even if we have been integrated with the clear light. When we sleep in this state, we do not experience sleep in darkness, like most ordinary minds. Instead, we sleep in clear light awareness. Everything is unified into the clear light devoid of any form of imagery, the practitioner's mind, and the essence of sleep itself. It is just like light falling into the light. Soon, when you have developed the ability to maintain awareness in this clear light, then even the uprising of dreams will not affect or distract you in any way. These kinds of dreams are known as clear light dreams, and they are entirely different from dreams of transparency and recurring samsaric dreams. In dreams generated in clear light awareness, there is no darkness or some sort of fuzziness.

All the supposed descriptions of clear light are just the results of dualistic judgments of human imagination. In actuality, the state of clear light is that which cannot be described. Because there is no "you" to describe it, and there is no "it" to be described. That is, there is no subject-object interrelation in clear light awareness. The clear light is the root of the primordial mind appreciating itself. And one cannot fully know how it feels to experience the peacefulness and perfect happiness that arise when abiding in clear light awareness until one directly experiences it firsthand.

THE SLEEP OF IGNORANCE

This is the kind of sleep that most people fall into after an exhaustive day of tedious physical and mental activities. It is also known as deep sleep, or the sleep of complete darkness. Anyone who experiences this kind of sleep just plunges into the dark nothingness of the sleep and exists in no identity until consciousness is regained at the start of the waking period. This is the sleep of utmost ignorance: we repeat it night after night, vanishing into sleep and repeat the same process the next day.

The samsara is rooted in a lot of negative emotions, of which ignorance is a majority. We exist in the samsaric dimension; therefore, we feel reinforced in our samsaric essence whenever we fall into the sleep of ignorance.

This sleep appears to us as just dark emptiness, where we lose our conscious self and every sense of identity. Our ignorant nature is the sole cause of falling into a deep sleep. The other less significant causes may be the nature of the weather, time of sleep, or how tedious the day's activities were. The only indicator for this kind is sleep is that there is no sense of consciousness.

REGULAR SAMSARIC SLEEP

In this kind of sleep, the dreamer gets tossed around in an endless loop of delusions. There are many varying experiences in the regular samsaric dreams conditioned by the impact of karmic traces on the dreamer's mind. The dreamer may encounter experiences based on several emotional traces, like anger, despair, hopelessness, worry, fear, and do lots of things such as chat with other beings, witness horrifying scenes, or get involved in rituals. The dreamer may experience the emotional embodiment of each and any of the dimensions of existence. None of these events and feelings is under the dreamer's control; everything is shaped by the state of the dreamer's mind. Every event that arises in regular samsaric sleep is determined by the residual karmic traces resulting from the dreamer's response to past experiences.

When in a deep sleep, there is no feeling or sense of presence; that is, the conscious mind stops functioning. However, in regular samsaric sleep, the mind is present while sleeping because the karmic traces deposited in the mind must form and condition dreams that arise in this state.

Since the causes of deep sleep are factors associated with our bodies, and our perception and dualistic response to karmic manifestations of experiences give rise to dreams, we need to control how we use our body in the samsara and stabilize the mind to get rid of dualism. This way, we stand a greater chance of succeeding in sleep yoga.

CLEAR LIGHT SLEEP

This is the ultimate realization in sleep yoga. It is also known as the sleep of transparency. We achieve this state through the practices of sleep yoga. When the practitioner sleeps, they do so in absolute presence, abiding in uninterrupted awareness. Neither the darkness of the deep sleep nor the dreams that arise in regular samsaric sleep are capable of distracting the practitioner. The practitioner keeps themselves in a pure state of clear light transparency and not carried about by the distractions of dreams as in regular samsaric sleep.

The clear light used in this context refers to the unification and oneness of the practitioner's energy in the central pranic passage. This results in the practitioner maintaining the state of non-dual awareness throughout their period of sleep. When we sleep, we do so with regard to the activeness of the body and mind. In clear light sleep, however, we sleep while in the state of rigpa, that is, pure awareness. Nothing matters but the clear light, which is the unification of the body and the conventional nature's mind.

When one dissolves in rigpa, thoughts and emotions will arise, as realized in earlier chapters. Immediately these thoughts arise, they dissolve into nothingness, leaving the practitioner in the pure base of rigpa. This does not mean that rigpa and the supposed practitioner are two separate entities. Once again, there is no subject-object relation between the practitioner and clear light in which they abide. There is no way to explain how this really is, but it is good to make instances. Air and wind, for instance, are practically the same thing, but under certain circumstances, we may use them in separate forms. We do this just to simplify the concept further. In reality, the rigpa is inseparable from a practitioner who dissolves in it. We only create the mirage of separation.

Practical Teachings Of Sleep And Dream

There are many similarities between sleep and dream practices. However, the significant difference between them is that, in dreams practice, the practitioner is still in the state of relating to some entity or phenomena as the object, in correspondence to him/her, the subject. While in sleep practice, there is only the maintenance of non-dual awareness. When working towards attaining the non-dual state of rigpa, dream yoga practices become some sort of preliminary practice because they are still associated with imagery, visual, and mental experiences. Whereas, in the practices of sleep yoga, there is no doer or recipient of an action. There is only the non-dual state of absolute rigpa.

At the beginning of the dream and sleep yogic practices, the student is usually first introduced to practices with form, spiritual activities involving qualities and characteristics that one can easily make sense of without having to experience it first. This is done to help the student progress from these simple forms of practice to the more sophisticated forms.

As expected, sleep practice is said to be more difficult than dream practices. The reason is not difficult to understand –in dreams, one could easily understand the teachings and follow the instructions. At the same time, in sleep practices, there is no precise or direct way to pass on instructions to the aspiring student. This is because, as stated earlier, the clear-light state of absolute rigpa cannot be described precisely with words. It can only be experienced. Also, our minds are more accustomed to phenomena bearing specific characteristics. So, we begin the dream and sleep practices with the practices that satisfy that condition.

Our identity is based on our minds' activities; therefore, we need some specific activities to support the mind during the beginning practices. Without much practice, when we try to become one with space all around, our minds play the trick of trying to envision a possible space region and melt with it: this is not the way of practice. But if, after sufficient practice and stability, one tries to utilize the features of objective experiences and the mind's stability to progress into the state of awareness with no features at all, then we say that the practice is going the right way.

For instance, if we are told to do something with a limited possibility, when we reach the point where we can no longer go on, it becomes clear to the practitioner as the state of emptiness. This is the kind of state we get when we count the English alphabets from "A" to "Z." Upon reaching the letter "Z," it becomes apparent that there is no more letter, but still, we need to continue. This sequence is similar to that which we encounter during practice. We literally start counting from "A" at the beginning of the practice, then the point of practice that we reach when we get to the letter "Z" is the point of the pure rigpa.

That way, we say that we have used the practices involving features and characteristics to attain the state of practice devoid of features or characteristics.

Unlike dream practices, the practice of sleep is formless, so there is nothing to focus on, whether substantial or not. The aim of the practice is the same as the practice itself. One has to integrate one's body and mind with the ultimate transparency and nothingness. The integration is not one based on dualism but one without any dualistic experience or response to those experiences. There is no you or it in this kind of practice, no old or new, no yes or no. In fact, there is no recognition of any dualistic behavior or concepts like time, limitation, or obstacle. Sleep practice is without any object or material on which to focus. This is the stage where the practitioner identifies and dissolves in the purity and emptiness of rigpa. In dreams, you regain your consciousness after alternating a series of sleep (loss of awareness) and dream as you progress in the cultivation of greater clarity in dreams. That is the main point of the dream: to mentally hold on to the dream and use it as an anchor or point of concentration to stay aware of the dream. Whereas, in pure sleep practices, we do not make use of any object or experience as an object of staying aware. Instead, we unite with the clear light transparency of absolute monism. This does not mean that we would be able to speak or even eat while simultaneously sleeping, for we would not. Our section of consciousness that deals with physical stimuli perception would have been deactivated while we sleep in absolute and non-dual clarity. With clear light awareness, it is like seeing without eyes or talking without a mouth.

After death, we will experience the intermediate state, bardo, in two phases. The first phase, known as the phase of conventional purity, is the most challenging stage to get liberated after death. Here, every experience based on the person's intuition dissolves into nothingness, the root of all essential experiences. At this point, we do not exist. Our presence becomes suppressed, just like it is in a deep sleep. We have no sense of perception whatsoever. Then, experiences start to form, and images start to appear, as dreams arise in recurring samsaric dreams. Then, once again, our sense of perception becomes laden with karmic dualism, and we tend to respond to those experiences dualistically. Karma, once again, takes over our experiences and condition our journey towards rebirth into another realm. If you are an accomplished sleep yogi with the ability to abide in clear light awareness, then you may be liberated in this phase of bardo.

After the first appearance of images and experience in the phase of conventional purity, the following stream of events is known as the next bardo. If a person fails to attain liberation in the first stage, it is in this phase that they will. In other words, if you are a master of sleep practice, then there is more probability of you attaining enlightenment in the phase of conventional purity. On the other hand, if you are not an accomplished sleep yogi but have mastered the dream practices, you will most likely attain liberation in the next bardo. But if you are not a master in either yogic practice, then you play along with the karmic dictations as you journey to your realm of rebirth.

The importance of sleep and dream yogic practices does not surpass each other. You only have to determine which one is best for you to master first. According to most traditional teachings, it is vital to recognize one's strengths and shortcomings before deciding which practice comes first. Asides from that, most people's minds are best suited for doing the practices of dreams before sleep practice. This is because not many people can cope with sleep practice's complexity without having experienced dream yoga beforehand. Another reason why it is advisable to begin with dream practices is that clarity in sleep practice takes a lot of time before it is fully developed when compared to clarity in dream yoga. And when one practices for so long without so much as an improvement, the outcome is usually a loss of confidence and enthusiasm, which, ultimately, can become a hindrance to smooth practice. Therefore, it is advisable to begin with dream practice, especially if your mind is a greatly dualistic one. This provides your mind with objects and events to grasp so as to make practice more accessible. After you have generated in yourself the capability to loosen your mind in monism, you may find it easier to practice sleep yoga. Just a touch of expertise is needed in either of the practices to strengthen oneself against impending obstacles.

There may be techniques and practices in dream practice that are different than that of sleep practice, but in the end, both practices end up on the same road. In dream practices, the practitioner's goal is to develop non-dual transparency in dreams to initiate clear-light dreams. When rigpa is attained, the practitioner begins to have several dreams based on the clear light. This eventually leads to the unification of the practitioner with and into the clear light. Also, in sleep yoga, the essence is to base the mind on clear-light sleep so that every dream that arises will be of clear light. Ultimately, the actual state of sleep is used to cleanse and stabilize the mind. In either case, the conclusive attainment requires one to become stable in the state of absolute rigpa both in the waking state and in sleep.

PART FIVE

PRACTICING SLEEP YOGA

The Guardian of Sleep

According to the tantric teachings, our sleep in the spiritual state is guarded and protected by a Dakini. The name of the dakini is Salgye Du Dalma (gsal-byed-gdos-bral-ma). The English translation of this is "She That Clarifies Beyond Conception." During practice, it is helpful to establish a relationship with her inherent nature. This is to receive blessings from her as we undergo the gradual process of transforming ignorance into lucidity because she makes up the light that illuminates the darkness of sleep.

In the individuality of sleep practice, this Dakini is formless. But when we start to fall asleep, we envision her as a ball of luminous light, a tiglé. Unlike during dream yoga practices, where we visualize luminosity in the form of Tibetan letters, we envision light in its pure state in sleep practices. This is because sleep practice is based on the level of subtlest energies, which cannot take a specific form or shape, and we are working on closing our minds against all sorts of dualistic mentality. Overcoming the habitual dualistic nature of the mind is a reasonably tricky task on its own because, when we try to envision something, the mind instinctively thinks of something, anything but itself. The sleep guardian, the Dakini, is the manifestation of the clear light. She is like us when we are in our actual, transparent state of luminous light. She is what we become when we perform dream practice.

Salgye Du Dalma is the essence of our most profound nature: the part of us we relate with when we practice in sleep. Also, it is helpful to remember her as much as possible during the day. This helps strengthen the connection we have established with the Dakini. In the daytime, she can be visualized as an entity of absolute whiteness, great luminosity, and immense beauty. She holds a hooked knife at the end of her right hand, and in the other, she holds a roughly hemispherical container made of a human skull. Her region of abode in the body is the heart area. She sits on a white circular moon.

The moon she is sitting on also rests on a golden sun disc, and the sun rests gracefully on a blue lotus of four distinct, beautiful petals. Like we did in the practice of Guru Yoga, envision yourself settling into her essence and her into yours. Mix your body and mind with her luminous essence until everything becomes one. You become the whiteness of her luminosity, and she is you that abides in a gentle calm and non-dual awareness.

This practice is somewhat similar to the practice of Guru Yoga. In both cases, you get to become the energy into which you are dissolving. Whenever you wake, let her wake within you; when you walk, know that she is walking with you; wherever you go, she is there with you. You can discuss with her and receive pieces of advice from her. Again, this is not about murmuring to yourself all day or doing crazy things. You can do all these with your ability to visualize. Imagine her instructing you on the things you already know. Make it a priority to think of her. When you do, allow her to remind you of maintaining non-dual awareness, exercise your leverage over negative emotions, and be wary of hindrances. You will not always have your spiritual master, nor will your friends always be available. But the Dakini will always be your guardian, you. Let her occupy the space of your time. Remember her constantly, and remain in awareness. Soon, whatever you do will begin to feel like you are doing it with her in your presence. When you talk to her, it feels as natural as though you were speaking to someone right next to you. She will personify all your knowledge and comprehension of the teachings and acknowledge them as a teacher would do.

If you remember her in a room, your body responds out of habit; it regains awareness and maintains it. Even your environment seems brighter and calmer than before. Your mind becomes greatly lucid and undistracted. Her presence will make you feel luminous and translucent. Then, alter your mind such that even distractions and the appearance of negativities remind you of her. By doing this, nothing can keep you from your non-dual awareness, and the negativities of the samsaric world only make you think of her.

For some people, this connection with Salgye Du Dalma may seem too fantastic or imaginative to be true. Then such people should apply the reasonable terms of human behavior with the practice. You may wish to hold her in awareness as a source of regaining awareness when it is lost or as an icon of distinct existence that you kind of remember all the time you need to make critical decisions. Either way, she should be your guardian and a cause for you to remain in awareness.

There is an immense ability to influence things in imagination which most people do not know. Imagination is powerful enough to confine one to the boundaries of the karma-conditioned samsara and is also sufficient to make genuine visualizations in the practice of spiritualism. A fair lot of humans waste their ability to envisage things on wasteful, samsaric matters. Instead of thinking about your quarrel with the next-door neighbor or the tests, you want to undergo the following week, why not take your time to envision this beautiful guardian of sleep who guides the consistent practitioners of sleep yoga. As usual, your intention of undergoing the practice is the first requirement in this process, like it is in every practice. Generate a firm intention of establishing a robust relationship between you and the base of your genuine nature, which is the exact meaning the Dakini portrays. Before you sleep, it is advisable to pray to her to attain clear light awareness. Prayer is a powerful feature of we humans that we do not know we have and consequently do not use. It is a source of hope and power when we get drained by hindrances and impediments. Thus, when you pray to the Dakini prior to sleep, your intention of achieving a high status in sleep practice becomes more powerful.

The Preparatory Practice

When one lives through a stressful day and then goes to bed at night, all the emotional pressure and tension will automatically be taken into sleep. So, if you can, dissolve your mind into rigpa, or, if you have not yet accomplished the dissolution into rigpa, then focus all your pranic composition on the central passage, and bring your awareness to the heart region. The practices of preparation that are advisable to undergo in dream practice are also applicable in sleep yoga. Connect with your icons of refuge. Merge with The Master as in Guru Yoga, or base your awareness on the Dakini, the guardian of sleep. It is also helpful to do the nine cleansing breaths to purge your mind of lingering negative karmic emotions. If you cannot do any of these by chance, you can prepare for the night by generating positive thoughts. If there are other exercises you do before going to sleep, it is all right; you can proceed with them.

Sleep practice is made more accessible by using a source of illumination to brighten up the sleeping area a little. A small lamp or a candle can be used for this purpose. It is meant to keep us in awareness. If you are using a candle, be careful of the exposed flame and take adequate measures to prevent a fire outbreak.

Keeping you in awareness is not the only function of the light; it also depicts the nature of the protective Dakini, Salgye Du Dalma. In the physical world, the only element closest to her nature of translucent is light itself. If you leave the light on and go to bed, envision this luminosity to be her essence standing above you, below you, and guarding your sleep on all sides. Allow the light to lead you into your own very luminous nature. Bring the state of external luminosity into the internal state, into you, the internal luminosity. Doing this, that is, using the physical world as an anchor, helps to make practice less complex for the mind. It creates an object -in this case, light- for the mind to hold on to while allowing yourself to abide in awareness.

One other procedure one can follow in preparation for the night is going without sleep for nights. This process is believed to weaken the ordinary mind and make it easier to find one's true nature without much difficulties or resistance from the conventional mind. If you decide to undergo this practice, you must first understand that you can either go one, three, or even five nights without sleep, although it is advisable to go one night without sleep at first. One other thing is that it must be in consecutive order. Also, make sure that you are doing this in the presence of a spiritual instructor you completely trust. After going sleepless for desired nights, when you finally fall asleep, the spiritual instructor is required to wake you up during the three waking hours of the night and inquire about the sleep from which you were woken. "Were you in awareness?" "Did you dream?" "Were you ignorant in sleep?" –these are the questions that the master asks the sleeper when he/she wakes. Each time the instructor wakes you, answer the questions you are asked, and go back to sleep. Do this three times during the night. That way, you will find your actual nature easier due to the ordinary mind's weakened state, which spawns distractions.

Main Practices During Sleep

In dream yoga, we wake during the night's four waking periods to undergo different dream practices. However, in sleep practices, we do the same practice in all four periods.

To begin, assume the lion position. This is done by lying, on the right side for men, while on the left side for women, as explained in previous chapters. Place the hand on the side with which you are lying down directly under your cheek. Then the hand on the upper side should be aligned downwards with the rest of the body. The legs should be bent forward so that the knees are almost level with the naval base. Then envision a beautiful blue lotus of four distinct, glorious petals in the heart region. At the center of the lotus is the Dakini, Salgye Du Dalma, in her elemental form: pure, transparent ball of luminous clear-light, a tiglé. Due to the blue color of the lotus's petals, the tiglé is visualized as being whitish blue, radiating blue light in every direction. Such is the luminosity of the tiglé. Afterward, merge your essence with the bluish light so that everything you see is the blue light. Dissolve into it and let it dissolve into you.

Once this is done, you will become one with the blue light; that is, you will be the clear blue light, and it will be you.

In addition to the tiglé at the center of the lotus, envision one tiglé resting on each of the four petals. On the front petal is a yellow tiglé. This one represents the east direction. The petal to your left side contains a green tiglé. This is the north direction. To your back is a red tiglé denoting the west direction. And to the right is the blue tiglé of the south direction. Each of these four tiglés denotes a Dakini in their clear-light form. You must not envision these dakinis in a different form other than in the form of balls of colored lights. The relationship between these dakinis and Salgye Du Dalma is similar to that of a group of warriors or nobles accompanying a king or other leader. Feel the presence of these protective dakinis around and within you. Maintain this developed sense of protection until you become calm and relaxed, knowing that there are dakinis to protect and guide you through the journey of sleep.

Make a prayer to the Dakini about the kind of sleep you want to fall into: in this case, the sleep of clarity. We are not referring to prayers taken with a pinch of salt. Instead, when you pray, do so with a deep sense of connection with the being to whom you are praying. Repeat this process several more times. Strong prayers help empower the essential requirement: the intent of the practice. A sense of powerful intention is required to break off the bondage of ignorance based on ordinary minds. Once you have become free from the basic mentality of ignorance, you can then discover your clear and luminous self.

FALLING ASLEEP

Entering sleep is a gradual process, but it is broken down into five stages in sleep practices. Doing this helps to undergo the entire procedure in awareness.

The only thing standing between consciousness and unconsciousness is our senses and our awareness of them. As we fall asleep, we slowly lose grasp of these senses, and sleep gradually overcomes the remaining bits of attention. This is the state of being unconscious. In sleep yoga, we use tiglés as a means of grasping onto consciousness when sleep starts to take over and the physical world starts dissolving. As the practitioner falls into sleep, they establish a connection with the five tiglés related to the progressive disappearance of the physical world. After the process, when the physical world has entirely gone blank, the practitioner goes into the absolute, non-dual awareness of clear light. The progression from one tiglé to another should be as smooth as silk. Also, it should be as unsegmented as the body of an ocean. This state should be maintained as we fall asleep and dissolve into non-dual awareness.

Stages of Sensory Withdrawal

From the moment we lie down to sleep to the time when we become unconscious of the external world, there are five phases of continuous sleep practice.

It begins when we assume the appropriate position for sleep practice. In this phase, you are still fully aware of your experiences. That is, you can see the light (if there is a light on), your ears can still hear, and you can still feel with your body. At this moment, you are in the state of Vision. The anchors of the ordinary mind are the experiences perceived by the senses. Then, slowly drift your consciousness towards the state of absolute awareness, which is the pure base of the tiglés. Firstly, bring your attention to the tiglé on the front of the body, and become one with its luminous yellow light. Then melt the awareness of the conventional mind with the yellow light, which represents the east direction, as stated earlier.

Then, after closing your eyes and the slight declination in the vividity of the physical world, your sense of Vision decreases. You start to lose your grasp on the anchor of the physical world. As this happens, bring your awareness to the green tiglé on your left side. Let the conceptual recognition of the ordinary mind dissolve with the loss of sensory perception as you merge with the green light of the North tiglé.

As your consciousness of the physical world becomes thinner, divert your awareness to the tiglé of the west direction. This tiglé faces the back of the body. The essence of the red light of this tiglé is to help you become present without any need for the physical anchors. With the help of this red tiglé, one's sense of conscious awareness does not dissolve with the sensory ability as one goes deeper into sleep.

When your perception of the external world is almost lost, shift your awareness to the blue tiglé of the south direction, and merge with it. This is the phase where you almost cease to feel. You lose virtually all your sense of awareness of the physical world. The blue tiglé faces the right side of the body, and its blue light helps your mind to remain in its understanding without any support from the external world.

Lastly, as you become fully asleep and all your sensory experiences have dissolved, bring your awareness into the central whitish-blue tiglé. In this stage, you should be able to abide in pure, clear light awareness, rather than using the central tiglé or the whitish-blue light to stay in awareness. Maintain clear light awareness in this state throughout the sleep period.

These five stages are not illustrative of our mental identities or our pranic settlements but the progressive dissolution of our perception of sensory experiences. Regularly, these processes take place in the unconsciousness of the sleeper's mind, but with practice, the practitioner undergoes these processes in awareness. The individual phases of the procedure should not be independently distinct. That is, the end of one step to the beginning of another should not be vivid. All the stages should seem like a single long practice. Let your awareness slide from the essence of one tiglé to another till there is nothing left other than the pure non-dual awareness, rigpa. You let your body into the state of peaceful sleep while you, in awareness, are allowed into the pure base of clear light. In shifting attention from one tiglé to another, it is not advisable to rely on conceptual instincts. Instead, we should integrate all the practice processes with the intent and let them unfold independently.

By chance, if you wake entirely in the middle of the practice, you should start all over again. As it always goes all one of the practices, you should always relax your body and calm your mind during this practice. If one stage of the procedure is taking too long, maintain the calm state of your mind. It does not matter how long a step takes. This specific practice unfolds differently for various people. Some people find it very easy to fall asleep while it takes long periods before others can finally sleep. The main point is, it is useless to try to be too neat with the practice. If it is all integrated into your mind, each stage will unfold without any visible effort. It is pointless to insist on being aware of which phase of the practice you are in or trying to make sure there is a distinction between each process. All these serve to distract you, and as a result, you lose grasp on the particular tiglé on which you are supposed to focus. You should understand the root and purpose of the practice and utilize it instead of allowing the mind to get distracted by the details.

It is also possible to initiate this practice with the tiglés in the opposite direction. The new organization would then be: the yellow tiglé in front and stands for the earth, the blue tiglé facing the right and stands for water, the red tiglé to the back, standing for fire, the green tiglé to the left, standing for air, and lastly, the whitish-blue in the middle, standing for space. This progression is comparable with the way the elements disappear in death. If you want to determine which sequence is best for you, that is all right.

This practice can be repeated when we wake during the night. We can sleep and wake at an approximately two-hour interval, as in dream practice. During each waking hour, determine your sleep qualities: were you aware? Were you in a deep sleep? Did you dream? Was it a samsaric dream? Or did you attain the state of clear light? Determine the aspect in which you are lagging and bear the intention to improve in your next wave of practice.

The Glowing Ball

There are many ways to define a tiglé, and each definition is suitable in various circumstances. In this specific practice, tiglé is a tiny ball of luminous light that portrays the rigidity of consciousness or, when visualized at the center of a lotus, represents absolute clear light awareness: rigpa. The luminous tiglé represents clear light that the mind grasps so as not to fall into unawareness. The light of the tiglés helps the mind focus in practice until one develops the ability to merge and become one with clear light. The essence of light is still substantial in the physical world. Its form is substantial only to a small extent, unlike other physical objects we use as anchors for the mind to grasp. So, the envisioning of luminosity as in tiglés is a means for the mind to practice until the mind no longer needs the light and abides in the calm and purity of the formless void of awareness pure light which is the base of the mind itself.

When you envisage the tiglés and their corresponding colors in the heart chakra, it is pointless to try and determine the precise location of the tiglés on each of the petals of the heart chakra's lotus. The point is to perceive, with your imagination, the central region in your heart chakra and instinctively find the appropriate place. This particular place is where you gain real experience.

In this practice and dream yoga, the particular color specified with each tiglé has its function. This means that these colors initiate different levels of excellence in the consciousness. They have a purpose of unifying these qualities with the qualities of the other actions in practice. These different levels of abundance of consciousness are observed as you shift awareness from one tiglé to another. The particular color of each tiglé also influences these changes. The consciousness senses the differences as one progresses into sleep, keeping the mind in awareness.

Unlike in dream practices, sleep yoga does not entail transforming feelings, emotions, or even identity. Instead, one's recognition of the conventional mind is abandoned as a whole. The mind is allowed to hold nothing in the imagination, other than the light: The light of the tiglés representing pure awareness. This is because if the luminosity is absent, the mind will be forced to grasp something else. So, we must keep it focused on the light until there is no need to hold on to anything anymore. That is the point when the mind becomes able to integrate the essence of light into itself, such that everything becomes the light, and the practitioner abides in pure, absolute rigpa, undistracted.

However, before the level of rigpa is attained, one finds it cumbersome to imagine how it is possible to remain in awareness without the mind grasping any form of object or visualization. Usually, when we say that we provide anchors for the mind, it means that consciousness needs an object to remain in awareness. So, the practices of dissolving the identity of the conventional sense are considered as a means of teaching the mind to become used to the absence of the customary dualistic engagements. They are making us ready for sleep yoga. In sleep yoga, we do not use any anchor for remaining in awareness. The essence of the practice is to merge the mind that relies on visualizations with pure awareness, in which case, there is no visualization and no practice.

Development In Practice

As one goes on with daily life activities with the ordinary mind, one often gets lost in thoughts of something else other than what is going on at the present moment. For instance, when one is busy (or supposed to be busy) at the workplace, one may get carried away, perhaps in thoughts of the pending bills, or of the imminent dinner with the girl at the subway, or about one's life as a whole. Then, when one becomes a spiritual practitioner, one becomes determined to remain in presence throughout the day's activities. When you walk, you do so in awareness. You incorporate everything you do and encounter into the practice and subsequently cultivate more awareness. However, doing this is not as easy as it seems because the mind is still wet with the moisture of dualism. The mind jumps around from one samsaric judgment to another, like an excited monkey, or worse. Then the practitioner brings it back to the object of awareness, where the mind stays aware for some time before it flies away in distraction again.

This is how the mind works with meditation, too. The mind remains in awareness with the help of the focusing object for some moment, then it gets distracted, and the practitioner brings it back to the object of attention. It usually takes a long time before awareness can be maintained for like, thirty minutes straight without any distraction.

When we start dream practice as well, this same sequence is recognized. In some dreams, we are lost; in others, we are lucid. Sometimes, we forget dreams, and sometimes, we do not. As we develop lucidity in dream practice, we start to spend longer lucid moments in dreams. Even with that, we may still lose ourselves in sleep. When we sleep, we may, once again, become lost in regular samsaric dreams and regain clarity. There may be alternating switches between non-lucid dreams and lucid dreams. As consistent practice is maintained and powerful intention is formed, we develop a stronger sense of awareness during dreams, and significant progress is made.

Although it is not this easy to make notable progress in sleep practices, very long periods of exercise should yield some recognizable results. If you do not perceive any noticeable results after long years of intense practice–no development in awareness, no positive changes in public life–you should consider this as an obstacle. Go to your teacher and perform the cleansing ritual. You may also need to search your mind for unfulfilled promises or agreements and fulfill them. Also, reorganize your pranic components with the sole aim of expelling obstacles and accomplishing higher levels in the sleep and dream yogic practices.

The gradual progression of the practitioner is similar to the growth of vine that only develops when there is something rigid to support it. The energies of the worldly components affect one's development in practice a great deal. Therefore, it is helpful to stay in places and associate with people that promote the practice. One may read meditational books, receive teachings, or hang out with other practitioners. All these behaviors help to develop in practice faster than when one does the opposite. Also, it allows one to identify obstacles more quickly and tackle them most appropriately.

Asides from the complexity of practice, practitioners are also faced with analyzing their lives to determine whether progress is being made in specific practices. If you ignore this process, you may continue to practice for years thinking that you are developing, when in actuality, there is no definite change.

Associated Hindrances

The concept "sleep yoga" does not necessarily mean the practices associated with sleep alone. The entire practice entails the observation of exercises that helps in abiding in awareness and dissolving the dualistic mind into the non-dual, pure state of rigpa. Sleep yoga consists of practices that guide the practitioner throughout the four states of internal and external existence: the waking state, sleeping state, meditation state, and death.

All the obstacles associated with these four states are all characteristic of diverting one away from the fruit of consistent practice: rigpa, and leading one into the dualism of the samsara. In correspondence to the four states of existence, the obstacles are:

a.   Failure to abide in awareness of the day's clear light due to distraction by a mental or physical perception of experiences.

b.   Failure to abide in awareness of sleep's clear light due to distraction by karmic dreams.

c.   Failure to abide in awareness of meditation's clear light due to distraction by thoughts and the mind's imagery.

d.   Failure to abide in awareness of the clear light in death due to the distraction by the sights and experiences of the bardo.

a.   *Failure to abide in awareness of the day's clear light.* Throughout waking life, the hindrances that we encounter are in the physical and external forms. We get distracted by the samsaric phenomena, the sights and occurrences, and our perception of them. When we hear a sound, we get carried away; that smell when it just finishes raining also steals away our awareness, and we get lost in anger at the person that bumped into us down the alley, making us fall prey to the call of sensory distraction.

However, when we abide in the non-dual awareness of rigpa, there is no distraction, just clear light. Our awareness is so deeply implanted in silence that no sound can distract us. Our awareness becomes so profoundly associated with the calmness that the sights and experiences of the samsara do not distract us.

There is no distinction between the clear light of the day and the night. However, the natural light is the clear light that of the day. Since both are connected, being able to abide in the clear light of the day helps attain rigpa during sleep. Therefore, the point is integrating one's sense of awareness into the clear light in the waking state, then, during sleep, and subsequently into the meditational state, until abiding in the form of rigpa becomes something that we can do easily.

b.   *Failure to abide in awareness of sleep's clear light.* The sole hindrance that impedes us from accomplishing the state of rigpa in sleep practices is the appearance of dreams. When we dream, we do so with our dualistic mind, relating with the phenomena of the dreams as an object with respect to the dreamer, the subject. This hindrance is also like the first, but in this case, it is internal. It is not actually the experiences of the dreams that block us from realizing clear light; our mind gets distracted from the path of attaining development. This is why the prayer we make at the beginning of the practice: that we have neither the deep sleep nor the sleep of samsaric dreams. Nevertheless, we continue to get distracted by dreams until we attain sufficient stability, at which point we begin to have clear light dreams.

c.   *Failure to abide in awareness of meditation clear light.* The clear light that is realized in meditation is called the clear light of presence. It is the accomplishment of the pure state of rigpa when meditating. In the preliminary meditation practices, thoughts are the impediments that block out practitioners from the clear light. When thoughts arise in the middle of meditation practice, we respond to them dualistically, and the mind gets driven off in distraction. However, when we have attained stability in rigpa, thoughts will arise and instantly dissolve in the non-dual awareness of the clear light.

The clear light of presence is not necessarily attained only after long periods of practice. The fact is, we can discover the clear light in ourselves at any point in time. One's knowledge of the conditions and requirements only makes the process easier.

d.   *Failure to abide in clear light awareness in death.* The hindrance that we encounter in the intermediate state after death (bardo) is the sights and experiences that arise in this state. The views do not, in themselves, stop us from attaining enlightenment during bardo. It is basically the mind that gets distracted by them. By responding to the after-death experiences in a dualistic manner, we get distracted from the pure transparency of rigpa. We stop reacting in a dualistic way to experiences when we embrace the clarity of clear light and abide in it.

The after-death visions are not supposed to affect the clear light in the state of bardo, nor are thoughts and mental imagery supposed to affect meditation clear light. Similarly, the physical waking life should not be influenced by the encounters with samsaric phenomena. The occurrence of distractive dreams should not control the clear light of sleep.

These four hindrances are the major obstructions that we need to overcome to attain freedom from samsaric sufferings and ignorance. After we have successfully reached the climax of sleep and dream practices, it will become easy for us to transform the hindrances and difficulties of the samsara into the path.

As mentioned earlier, the purpose of sleep practices is not confined to the process of sleep alone. It is for incorporating all the states of existence: waking, sleeping, meditating, and in bardo into the clear light. The only outcome of achieving this is enlightenment. Thoughts, feelings, fantasy, delusive imageries, or perceptions of experiences can appear in the practitioner's mind even in the state of rigpa. When this happens, let them dissolve abruptly into the clear light and the associated emptiness. This way, there would be no karmic trace to cause further karmic experiences. Every experience we encounter thereon will then become vivid, instant, and satisfying. We experience everything in presence; when we touch a flower, the mind stays on the flower; when we speak to someone, we do so in earnest awareness. Subsequently, all our experiences become integrated with the clarity and awareness of the clear light.

Practical Recommendations

The practices described here are recommended to support the significant sleep practice. Many of these practices are suggestions of the mother Tantra and are advised to sustain the primary practice in sleep yoga.

Devotion to the Master

This is done to help the practitioner discover and maintain the actual state of mind. Generate a strong sense of intention, then envision The Master abiding just at the top of your forehead, slightly higher than the forehead chakra. Then develop a tremendous commitment towards The Master. Your association with The Master should be of pure, transparent, and non-dualistic devotion. During envisaging the Master, abide in pure awareness and do not just visualize The Master's image. Allow yourself to get drawn to the essence of the Master, which is the pure, transparent root of your primordial mind. Make honest and powerful prayers of devotion to the Master, and tender your appreciation for the knowledge of teachings you have been privileged to encounter.

After doing that, then imagine The Master dissolving into pure, luminous light. The light merges with you by entering through your forehead and into your heart. Imagine The Master remaining as transparent in your heart, abiding there in great calm. Allow this calmness to flow over your entire body in waves of peaceful apprehension. Then go to sleep.

The devotion you generate towards The Master is actually your devotion towards your actual state of mind.

Dependence on the Dakini

With your imaginative ability, envision the Dakini, Salgye Du Dalma, abiding on a silver, luminous moon disk, which in turn sits on a golden sun disk that sits above the lotus in the heart region. The Dakini abides in the heart region in her bright, transparent, and luminous form. Become aware of her powerful presence around and within you. Be aware of her love, empathy, and kindness. Know that she is your guide along the path to enlightenment at the very base of your mind. She is the only being whom you can completely trust. She is your protector, your aid in times of trouble. Her essence is the liberation from the samsara, the key to achieving your aim. Love her, depend on her, have complete trust in her powers and ability, and respect her essence within your heart. Pray to her in utmost focus, and see her as the brightness of the path, then go to sleep.

Conduct

Go somewhere quiet and make sure the place is clear of people who could distract you. In fact, make sure there are no people at all. Then, start releasing whatever feeling or emotion you have bottled up inside of yourself. You can act wildly if you have to. Shout, scream, cry, jump, or even undergo several emotional outbursts that could have been obstructing significant progress in your yogic practices. You need not be wary of your surroundings; remember that no one is near you. The purpose of the exercise is to purify you and purge your body of all emotional distress. Then make prayers to The Master or the Dakini, or offer a sacrifice to the buddha to revitalize your mind. After praying for the opportunity to experience the clear light, go to sleep.

Prayer

We should integrate the act of praying into each of our practices. When you do not make any notable progress during a specific procedure, pray consistently for that progress. Humans find it difficult to understand the power of prayers. We believe that prayers are qualities aimed at some entities other than ourselves, but the truth is, we only need to maintain a strong need and powerful intention in the prayer.

Usually, it is part of human behavior to react to whatever is said to us. When someone always sweetly talks to us, we get flattered, and our inclination towards the person deepens. Similarly, when we get spoken to harshly, we feel bad. That is the point: we are likely to be more successful in practice if we always remain positive, and we can do this by staying around people who encourage us. The progress in practice becomes impeded when we start to promote negativities by being with people whose mouths do not say positive things. In short, it is vital to be positive at all times and to pray, not only in times of difficulties but also to achieve greater heights in the practices of sleep and dream yoga.

Also, your prayers should be made with powerful levels of intention. Do not pray with the same intensity with which you speak casually. Put all your strength and feelings of transparency into your prayers. After praying fervently, expect your results in good faith, and go to sleep.

The merging

Here, we are concerned with merging the bright, radiant light with the essence of the practitioner. Of course, it is not that easy. One has to master the exercise of focusing and maintaining concentration on a specific mental object of practice which, in this case, is the bright, pure blue light.

To begin, calm down and loosen all tensions formed as a result of dualistic experiences. Close your eyes firmly, then imagine the whitish-blue tiglé in the heart region. The tiglé should be about the size of a small almond. Then, still abiding in the absolute calmness, gently expand the light of the tiglé. See, with your mind's eye as it covers more areas, first consuming your whole heart and then stretching out further. It is not enough to just envision the whitish-blue light; perceive it with your body instead. Let the light spread out further and continue to perceive it in glorious waves. Then picture the light dissolving everything it contacts. Let the light turn everything to nothingness: your whole body, the room in which you are practicing, the entire house, your city, your entire country, and the entire world.

As the light dissolves everything, allow your feelings and emotions to be included. Let the light cleanse you of dualism and dissolve every dualistic desire. Once everything has turned to light on the outside, then let the light fill you up again. Then dissolve all of your internal events in the light. Then your body becomes nothing but the whitish-blue light. All your problems and difficulties, gone: dissolved in the light. Then, there is no distinction between you and the blue light. There is no external or internal, no you, or it. There is only the blue light, abiding in calm awareness. Everything, every distraction of the physical world no more exists. You should not be all tensed up in concentration as you go through with this. As mentioned earlier, remain in absolute calm as you dissolve all experiences into the light. When this is done successfully, integrate the blue light into vast space—the space of the heart. Then go to sleep.

The 'HUNG' practice

This practice is almost the same as the *merging* practice discussed above, only that the 'HUNG' practice is more traditional. As you exhale, imagine countless radiant blue Tibetan syllable HUNG spontaneously flowing out through each of your nostrils. Using your imagination, feel as they appear in the heart region, rise to the head through the energy channels, and get expelled through your nostrils with each breath. Afterwards, as they come out through your nostrils in great numbers, the blue HUNGs dissolve everything they touch, spreading the blue light in all directions. They spread out further and dissolve everything in existence. At this point, there is nothing around you but the blue HUNG. Then allow the light of the syllable to flow back to you–to your body and mind, and dissolve in it. Then, remain in the non-dual awareness. The minimum number of breaths for this practice is twenty-one, but you can do more if you feel up to it. This practice is most suitable during the day, and it is helpful to perform it as frequently as possible.

Your mind may be unwilling to accept the fact that there is neither a subject nor a corresponding object in this practice. Therefore, one must have developed the ability to abide in the pure state of rigpa before attempting this practice. As you exhale those HUNG syllables, they dissolve everything that you perceive, and you, the perceiver. Everything external and internal becomes nothing but HUNG syllables of great luminosity. You become the light; the light becomes you. Your mind may try to fly away in distraction, and it will. When it does, allow the specific object of distraction to be dissolved in the blue HUNGs. Then the mind regains its awareness in the subjective state, when it does, dissolve it, too. Do this continuously, and you will be able to dissolve the feeling of rigidity. Nothing is either here or there, and everything becomes the blue HUNG.

Unification Of Rigpa

The sole purpose of attaining the state of rigpa through sleep and dream yoga is to unify it with all the attributes of life. Our lives must be of a specific status. There are two possible options: we can either determine the shape and condition of our lives by ourselves or leave everything for the forces of karmic manifestations to decide, which is undoubtedly a terrible idea. When we begin to unify the practice of the teachings with life, our lives start changing for the better.

Unifying the clear light with the three venoms

The three venoms: unawareness, appetition, and antipathy, form the base upon which other negative emotions are built. To enhance positivity in life, we must unify these three venoms with clear light.

Getting rid of the first basic venom, unawareness, is the principal objective of sleep yoga. Using sleep yoga as a medium and the clear light as the source of power, we destroy ignorance and dissolve the mind into clear light awareness.

Appetition is a major obscuration from discovering our true selves. Unaware, we get so lost in desire that we become unable to attain the state of rigpa. The sense of appetition arises from the feeling of lack of something, which occurs as a result of our dualistic experiences. When we lack something that we feel will be advantageous to us, we generate a feeling of want, which ripens into desires. All these do not exist in the pure state of rigpa. But to achieve rigpa itself, one must have developed a feeling of desire, which is, of course, the most selfless and transparent of desires.

Appetition, on its own, is not difficult to liberate. But one does not generate a desire without an object of interest. In the procedure of discharging appetition, one must focus on the arising desire directly without attaching the specific object of interest. This way, we can dissolve appetition at its base. Following this, the thing of interest also dissolves spontaneously, and so do you, the supposed subject. Only then can one realize the clear light awareness.

The moment of satisfaction that occurs when we fulfill a desire can also liberate the mind.

When you satisfy yourself with something you desire, the feeling of desire stops, and the root of dualism between you and the object of interest disappears. You then become momentarily free from the distractive sense of longing. This exact moment is a moment of truth when you can quickly discover your actual self without much practice. But as soon as we satisfy one dualistic desire, we get carried away once more by the dualism of karmic forces.

The deep and small pleasures we derive from satisfying our desires create a broader chance for developing the ability to discover one's state of mind in its true form. So, instead of just getting carried away in pleasure that will eventually result in nothingness, we can abide in non-dual awareness while at the same time enjoying the pleasure of satisfying one's desire. This does not mean that when we remain in awareness when fulfilling an appetition, we will be immune to the joy of pleasurable desires. When we combine the clear light transparency with the eventual emptiness of pleasures, then we will feel the joy that arises with pleasure but will not allow it to distract us from the pure, clear light awareness. This approach is not restricted to a specific experience. We can utilize pleasure to practice in clear light and combine transparency and nothingness, which subsequently gives rise to joy and pure awareness.

Negative emotions such as feelings of hatred or anger can also be addressed similarly. To liberate the negative emotions that we feel for someone or something, we need not remain aware of the negativity still bottled up internally. Instead, we should address the feeling singly without forming any link or recognition with it. This makes it easy to dissolve the negative emotion into clear light awareness, which is you of absolute truth and wisdom.

Unification with the time cycles

Usually, when we describe a practice, we do so in relation to opinion, meditation, and human conduct. Here, the procedure is concerned with the concept of human behavior or conduct. The idea of behavior is defined in terms of integrating time cycles with inner and outer energies.

We consider it a typical experience to feel more fatigued as the day progresses. That is, we become less energetic as time passes. In this practice, the passage of time will help us stabilize our clear light experience further.

-The Outer Unification: Unifying the Clear Light with the Experiences of Day and Night

To begin this practice, we need to divide the twenty-four hours of the day into distinct lengths of time that we can use to develop further our stability concerning the pure experience of clear light. In ancient times, people set the day into distinct periods using the natural indications of day and night, but we cannot apply this method anymore. It is not exactly favorable to people whose schedules are different. Moreover, the time of the day does not necessarily affect the instruction's influence in our lives, as discussed in the teachings. According to the Mother Tantra, we divide the day and night into four separate periods as follows:

1. Developing conscious awareness.
2. Awareness during sleep
3. Waking with the natural mind
4. Maintaining pure presence during the waking state.

Developing conscious awareness

This is the first of the four periods, and it is believed to be between sunset and before going to bed. In the late evening, to be precise. This is when all the actions of the day have led to exhaustion, for the people who work during the day, at least. One's sharpness at the start of the day has been weakened by the stress of the day's activities. In this period, the senses, both internal and external, become dull and less powerful. This phenomenon can be compared to the illustration of many small rivers streaming along to join a larger body of water. The small rivers are the thoughts, ideas, emotions, perception, the senses, all pouring into nothingness. But we need not let our awareness dissolve with our thoughts into the darkness of sleep. We can become the sea–the larger body of water into which everything dissolves into emptiness. Therefore, instead of going towards the state of blank unconsciousness that is the significant characteristic of exhaustion, we can integrate our awareness with the clear light and maintain the pure presence that arises throughout the first period.

Tibetan Yoga Academy

Maintaining awareness during sleep.

This period follows the first and is considered to be between the moment you go to sleep to the time you wake for another day. In ancient times, the ending time for this period is at dawn. This period is characterized by absolute calmness and silence, which makes the practice easily doable.

Your sleeping time should not just be a period of blank unawareness filled with confusion and ignorance caused when karmic dreams arise. Also, awareness is not just developed spontaneously in sleep without any sense of intention or effort. You have to start cultivating awareness from the time you wake and throughout the day in order to make it easy to remain present in sleep. When sleep finally comes, and feelings, thoughts, and other mental distractions have disappeared with the deactivation of the ordinary mind, you should remain in pure presence. This state is very close to the state of nirvana. In nirvana, there is a cessation of all samsaric sufferings–the realization of ultimate bliss.

Maintain this state until you wake in the morning.

Waking with the natural mind

This is the third period, and it is considered to begin when you wake from sleep, preferably at dawn, till the sun rises. At this point, the mind is fully refreshed, and the day proceeds on a new note–the first light of the day is appearing, and the fantastic elements of nature are in the freshest form. On the inner side, one experiences the transition between sleep's stillness and quiet and the full commencement of the day's activities.

As stated earlier, it is advisable to wake early, preferably just before dawn. Arise in the morning in the actual state of mind instead of the ordinary mind. This is a bit easier to do at the specific moment because the ordinary mind is not entirely awake yet. Try to abide in non-dual awareness where there is no subject-object discrimination. Experience all the phenomena that arise in this period without recognizing yourself as the subject. Simply observe everything in clear light awareness, and generate a firm intention for the next practice.

Maintaining pure presence during the waking state

This is the last period and the fourth. It starts with your full engagement with the day's activities and ends when the sun goes down.

In this period, the mind is working at its full capacity, actively sorting through ideas, thoughts, feelings, and emotions. We interact with other people, and our pranic components also influence us as we progress through the day. Despite the full busyness of the mind and body at the start of the waking period, we should remain in non-dual awareness of clear light. Suppose we integrate the state of rigpa into all of our experiences during the day. In that case, we observe every experience and emotion that arises with absolute monism, without any sense of dualism whatsoever. This helps us to make more positive choices and decisions.

Generally, these practices of integrating rigpa with the conditions and experiences of day and night have the purpose of helping us discover and maintain our true nature. When this happens, we unlock the advantages that come with the truth and wisdom of the primordial base of the mind.

The Inner Unification: Unifying the clear light with sleep

The sequence of the practices in this division is somewhat like the first division, only that the inner unification is not based on a twenty-four-hour procedure. Here, we are concerned with the observation of constant awareness throughout one interval of the day, and one interval of sleeping time, whether we are sleeping for a whole night or a few hours.

Generating the intention to practice is also very vital for this specific practice. Furthermore, we should see the ability to practice the teachings in general as an opportunity and be grateful for it. If we perceive the whole idea of practice as a worrisome responsibility, it is best not to do it at all. We should practice the instructions in the teachings only if there is sufficient intent and a genuine desire to practice.

Like the first section, this section is also broken down into four periods. These are the periods:

- Prior to sleep
- After sleep

- After waking, but before we get preoccupied with the day's busyness
- Of being active up to the following time of sleep

The period before sleep

The first section is the period between the time we lie down to sleep and the time we fall asleep. In this period, all thoughts and experiences dissolve into emptiness.

The period after sleep

In this section, one's senses have been consumed by the emptiness of sleep. The purpose of identity is then lost following this phenomenon. In this phase, one is left with innate awareness.

The period after waking

The mind is still in the state of total transparency, made better due to the fuzziness of the ordinary sense.

The period of being active

At this point, the dualistic mind will have fully awakened, and thoughts, karmic experiences, and samsaric distractions begin to arise. But still, the non-dual transparency of the clear light is maintained. We then undergo the trials and sufferings of the samsara in the pure state of rigpa, in which case they get dissolved into nothingness.

Hidden Unification: Unifying the Clear Light with the Intermediate State (Bardo)

This practice is concerned with the unification of the clear light with the bardo. Dying, we have learned, is a bit like falling asleep. Therefore, this section is also broken down into four sections, just like the previous sections.

1.   Disintegration
2.   Origination
3.   Encounters
4.   Unification

Disintegration

This is the first procedure we undergo after death. The various componential constitutions of the body start to decompose and dissolve. The pranic components escape the body, emotions dissolve, and so do the energy of life and consciousness.

Origination

After the body decomposes, the stages of bardo commence. The first bardo, the bardo of original purity, is known as the origination. Just like sleeping, this period is also characterized by the absence of the conscious mind. If a practitioner practiced vividly while still alive, they would find it easy to get rid of dualism at this stage and attain liberation into clear light.

Encounters

Following the state of origination bardo, the after-death experiences start to arise. As with dreams in dream yoga, shapes, images, and figures start to emerge. With the help of dualism, virtually everyone will recognize some of these images and respond to them dualistically, leading to more cycles of karmic events. Only a successful sleep and dream yogi will get liberated in this stage.

Unification

This stage is called the bardo of empirical reality. If a practitioner has profound experience in the yogas of sleep and dream, they would realize the absolute truth within this intermediate state. But suppose the practitioner has not developed stability in the practices of dream and sleep. In that case, they get attached to the delusional visions that arise and react to them in a dualistic manner. By doing so, they earn themselves a rebirth in one of the six realms of suffering.

CONCLUSION

Usually, these practices are not standard in Tibet. They are somewhat secret teachings that are not exposed to just anyone. But now, all that is in the past. Time has changed, and circumstances have changed with it. The teachings need to be available to the general public so that people may have access to something sacred that might improve our understanding of how dreams work.

Throughout the period of receiving and practicing the teachings, some people may view the teachings as some sort of responsibility that cannot be lifted. This should not be so. The teachings should be seen as a means of treading the path to truth and wisdom. The teachings are not a burden if one discovers how to apply them in the right parts of our lives.

Furthermore, do not use yourself as a slave to practice. Do not just practice without the intent required for the procedure. Understand the essence of the course and do it without allowing it to become detrimental to your personal life.

The practices of sleep yoga are more challenging to attain than dream practices. In ancient writings discovered during the compilation of the teachings, accomplished yogic masters have written that it took them several years of constant exercise to achieve results in sleep practice particularly. So, do not be discouraged if you do not notice any results despite all your efforts. Every attempt you make counts as something, as long as you do not consider the practice as a burden and practice it with joy and good intentions. Even if you are still yet to achieve notable results during sleep itself, you do have the advantage of increased awareness. That is also good for your daily life and practice.

This book is written with the purpose of helping people to find a new reality in dreams and sleep and for leading new practitioners into a life of great spiritualism and more minor samsaric difficulties. So, good luck!

Made in the USA
Middletown, DE
16 October 2023

40885799R00154